Henry Francis Walling

The Morris and Essex R. R.

And the Anthracite Coal Regions of Pennsylvania

Henry Francis Walling

The Morris and Essex R. R.
And the Anthracite Coal Regions of Pennsylvania

ISBN/EAN: 9783337080440

Printed in Europe, USA, Canada, Australia, Japan

Cover: Foto ©ninafisch / pixelio.de

More available books at **www.hansebooks.com**

Taintor's Route and City Guides

Pennsylvania Coal Regions,
VIA
Morris & Essex R. R.

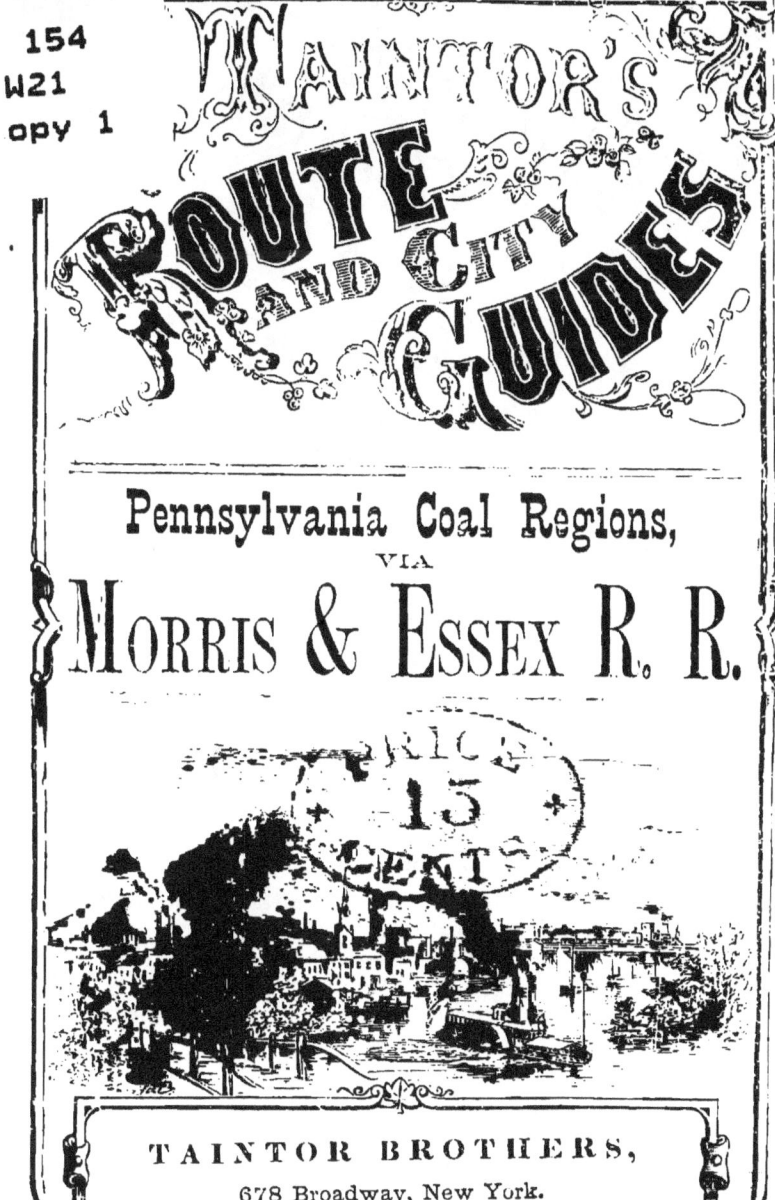

PRICE 15 CENTS

TAINTOR BROTHERS,
678 Broadway, New York.

Economy only second to Security.

Atlantic Mutual Life Insurance Company.

ALBANY, N. Y.

SPECIAL ADVANTAGES.

Ten per cent. reduction from rates to practical Homœopathists.

Annual Division of Profits.

Immediate Payment of Losses.

All Policies Incontestable and Non-forfeitable.

Liberal Provisions to Travelers.

AND BY SPECIAL ACT,

The value of its Registered Policies is deposited with the State of New York.

This Company offers liberal inducements to first-class Agents. It will always render them the most substantial tokens of appreciation, and afford them every encouragement in sustaining a successful and honorable competition.

Officers:
ROBERT H. PRUYN, President.
JAMES HENDRICK, Vice-President.
LOUIS B. SMITH, Secretary.

SEND FOR A CIRCULAR.

All men think all men mortal but themselves.

Insure while in health; the sense of security is worth the cost.

Insure Now! Present action will secure future comfort.

PHŒNIX
Mutual Life
Insurance Company
HARTFORD, CONN.

Assets, November 1, 1868,
OVER
$3,500,000.

The following are some of the advantages offered by this Company:

Its Policies are the freest from restrictions as to travel, residence, and employment, of any company in the land. Its premiums are as low as those of any safe company. Its dividends have been uniformly 50 per cent. during last four years. Its dividends are always based on full premium paid. It charges no extra premium on lives of females. It offers all the advantages of a Cash and Note Company. It is prompt in settling all just claims.

That the public appreciates these advantages, is manifest from the following

TABLE OF COMPARISONS OF THE BUSINESS,
For the year ending June 15, 1868, with the Business for the year preceding, of the PHŒNIX MUTUAL LIFE INSURANCE COMPANY.

Number of Policies issued during year,..........................7,167
Number of Policies issued during previous year,................4,331
    Increase,..................................2,836
  Rate of increase, 65 per cent.

Amount insured during year,..............................$19,685,254
Amount insured during previous year,......................10,792,749
    Increase,.............................$8,892,505
  Rate of increase, 82 per cent.

Income for the year,....................................$1,445,211 50
Income for the previous year,..............................914,882 60
    Increase,..........................$530,328 90
  Rate of increase, 58 per cent.

Assets June 15, 1868,...................................$2,992,840 11
Assets June 15, 1867,....................................1,746,507 72
    Increase,........................$1,246,332 39
  Rate of increase, 71 per cent.

Received from Interest, 1868,.............................$146,808 33
Paid in Losses, in 1868,...................................114,140 34
Showing that the Company received..........................$32,667 99
  more from interest than it paid in losses.

INSURE IN THE "PHŒNIX MUTUAL," OF HARTFORD, CONN.

J. F. BURNS,   E. FESSENDEN,
Secretary.   *President.*

New York Agency, 153 Broadway.   Boston Agency, 134 Washington St.
Albany   " 443 Broadway.   Philadelphia " 430 Walnut St.

HOMŒOPATHIC
Mutual Life Insurance Company
OF THE CITY OF NEW YORK,
No. 231 BROADWAY.

Rates Lower than any other State or National Company.

HOMŒOPATHISTS LOWER STILL.

Why pay twice as much as is necessary to insure, merely to let the company *bank* on your money and pay you back in dividends?

Dividends to a reasonable extent guaranteed in advance by deduction from premiums.

All premiums, policies, and dividends in cash.

LADIES, LOOK AT THIS!

Females insured at same rates as *males*. All policies non-forfeitable. All dividends non-forfeitable.

Call or send for Documents.

DIRECTORS.

D. D. T. MARSHALL, 157 East 34th Street.
Hon. S. L. WOODFORD, Lieut.-Gov. State New York.
JAMES CUSHING, JR., of Leroy W. Fairchild & Co.
EDWARD E. EAMES, of H. B. Claflin & Co.
ELISHA BROOKS, of Brooks Brothers, 468 Broadway.
Hon. R. B. CONNOLLY, Comptroller of N. Y. City.
ROBERT SEWELL, of Sewell & Pierce, 62 Broadway.
GEORGE G. LAKE, of Lake & McCreery, 471 Broadway.
Hon. RICHARD KELLY, Pres't of 5th National Bank.
JOHN SIMPKINS, 20 Wall Street.
W. C. DUNTON, of Bulkley, Dunton & Co., 4 John St.
PETER LANG, of Lang & Clarkson, 4 Front Street.
W. B. KENDALL, of Bigelow Carpet Co., 65 Duane St.
H. W. WARNER, late Warner & Loop, 332 Fifth Ave.
CHARLES L. STICKNEY, 209 Bowery.
WILLIAM RADDE, Publisher, 550 Pearl Street.
THOMAS B. ASTEN, 124 East 29th Street.
G. B. HAMMOND, Tarrytown, N. Y.

D. D. T. MARSHALL, President.
JAMES CUSHING, JR., Vice-Pres't.
E. A. STANSBURY, Secretary.
A. HALSEY PLUMMER, Ass't Secretary.
STEWART L. WOODFORD, Counsel.
EDWIN M. KELLOGG, M.D., } Medical
JOHN W. MITCHELL, M.D., } Examiners.
A. COOKE HULL, M.D., Medical Director.

GENERAL AGENTS.

RYNALL & CLEVELAND, 231 Broadway, New York and New Jersey.
DR. JOHN TURNER, 725 Tremont Street, Boston, for Maine and Massachusetts.
JOSEPH M. WOOD, Wrentham, General Agent for Massachusetts.
EDWIN HEDGES, Traveling Agent for Vermont and New Hampshire.
CHARLES G. WIGHTMAN, Bristol, Conn.
A. M. WARD, 220 Chapel Street, New Haven.
S. H. STAFFORD, Marietta, Ohio, for the States of Ohio and West Virginia.
P. H. EATON, 343 F Street, Washington, D. C.
ED. W. PHILLIP, 59 Second Street, Baltimore, Md.
JOHN W. MARSHALL, Aurora, Illinois, for North-western States.

Agents and Solicitors wanted.   ☞ Send for Circular.

HOME
LIFE INSURANCE COMPANY,
254 Broadway, New York.

Assets, $2,000,000 (increasing rapidly). 10,000 Members.

In every respect a sound, first-class institution. Just such as a prudent man would select as the depository of the funds designed for those he is to leave behind him.

Policy Holders receive all the Profits.

Dividends annual, on the contribution plan.

This Company has declared and actually paid, a dividend to its Policy holders every year since its organization.

No restriction in its Policies as to residence or travel in any part of the world.

One-third the premium may, if desired, remain as a permanent loan, to be paid by the dividends.

No Policy or other fees charged, and no extra premium on Females.

SEND FOR CIRCULAR.

WALTER S. GRIFFITH,   *GEO. C. RIPLEY,*
President.   *Secretary.*
ISAAC H. FROTHINGHAM,   WM. J. COFFIN,
Treasurer.   *Actuary,*

GOOD AGENTS WANTED.

Charter Oak Life Insurance Company,

HARTFORD,   CONN.

ASSETS   ANNUAL INCOME

$5,250,000,   *$3,250,000,*

and rapidly   and constantly

increasing.   enlarging.

Policies issued, nearly 40,000. Losses paid, $1,750,000. Dividends paid, $1,500,000. Annual dividends paid, commencing with first renewal.

J. C. WALKLEY, Pres.   Z. A. STORRS, Vice-Pres.
S. H. WHITE, Sec'y.

N. S. PALMER, Gen'l Agent for N. Y. City, 183 Broadway.
HILLIARD BROS., Gen'l Agents for Philadelphia, 415 Walnut St.
E. H. BLAIR, Gen'l Agent for East'n Penn., Williamsport, Penn.

WALLING'S ROUTE AND CITY GUIDES.

These GUIDES describe all CITIES, TOWNS and STATIONS on the routes, giving items of interest to the traveler for business or pleasure, and

HANDSOMELY COLORED AND VERY PERFECT MAPS,

enabling the traveler at every part of his journey to mark his precise locality, and recognize the surrounding scenery.

ALSO,

TIME TABLES OF RAILROADS

AND

STEAMBOATS.

The following GUIDES are already published:

- I.—WALLING'S "CITY OF NEW YORK" GUIDE.
- II.—WALLING'S HUDSON RIVER GUIDE.
- III.—WALLING'S NEW YORK CENTRAL GUIDE.
- IV.—WALLING'S ERIE RAILWAY GUIDE.
- V.—WALLING'S SPRINGFIELD ROUTE GUIDE.
- VI.—WALLING'S SHORE LINE ROUTE GUIDE.
- VII.—WALLING'S LONG ISLAND SOUND GUIDE.
- VIII.—WALLING'S NEW YORK TO WASHINGTON ROUTE GUIDE.
- IX.—WALLING'S HARLEM ROUTE GUIDE.
- X.—WALLING'S CONNECTICUT RIVER AND WHITE MOUNTAINS GUIDE.
- XI.—WALLING'S NEW JERSEY CENTRAL R.R. AND ALLENTOWN LINE.
- XII.—WALLING'S MORRIS AND ESSEX AND COAL REGIONS GUIDE.

FOR SALE BY BOOK AND NEWS DEALERS.

TAINTOR BROTHERS, Publishers,

No. 678 BROADWAY, NEW YORK.

WALLING'S "CITY OF NEW YORK."

Contains descriptions of, and directions for visiting the PUBLIC BUILDINGS, PARKS, CEMETERIES, ISLANDS, and PUBLIC INSTITUTIONS in and around New York City; also, contains lists of the principal Hotels, Places of Amusement, Libraries, Clubs, Societies, Dispensaries, Horse Railroads, Omnibus Routes, Hack Fares, Ferries, &c.; also,

A NEW STREET DIRECTORY,

TRAVELERS' DIRECTORY AND CHURCH DIRECTORY,

AND A

LARGE COLORED MAP

OF

NEW YORK, BROOKLYN, JERSEY CITY, HOBOKEN, &c.

Price, 25 cents. For Sale by Newsdealers and Booksellers.

TAINTOR BROTHERS, Publishers,

No. 678 BROADWAY, NEW YORK.

PHELPS, DODGE & CO.,

13 to 21 CLIFF STREET, NEW YORK,

IMPORTERS AND DEALERS IN

TIN PLATES,   ROOFING PLATES,
    SHEET IRON,   COPPER,
      ZINC,   WIRE,
        BRASS,   LEAD, AND
         PIG TIN.

BRAMHALL, DEANE & CO.,

247 & 249 WATER STREET,

NEW YORK.

Hotel Ranges & Furniture

A SPECIALTY.

ÆTNA LIFE INSURANCE COMPANY,
OF HARTFORD, CONN.

This old and reliable Company issued
Over 15,000 Policies during the Year 1867,
and received over
FIVE MILLION DOLLARS INCOME.

(*Extract from the New York Independent.*)
"Among the substantial and enterprising institutions of Hartford, Conn. the Ætna Life Insurance Company stands prominent."

(*Extract from the Insurance Monitor.*)
"No Life Insurance Company ever achieved so complete a success as this popular institution. Its prosperity is a together *unprecedented* in the annals of commercial enterprise in this country.
The Ætna is a Company that can be thoroughly trusted. It is sound, prompt, and progressive."

E. A. BULKELEY, *Pres't.* AUSTIN DUNHAM, *Vice-Pres't.*
T. O. ENDERS, *Sec'y.*

INSURE YOURSELF AGAINST
ACCIDENTS OF TRAVEL
BY TICKETS ISSUED BY THE
Railway Passengers' Assurance Co.
OF HARTFORD, CONNECTICUT.

J. G. BATTERSON, Pres't. H. T. SPERRY, Secretary

THE

Morris and Essex R.R.,

AND THE

Anthracite Coal Regions

OF

PENNSYLVANIA.

WITH

SKETCHES OF CITIES, VILLAGES, STATIONS, SCENERY, AND OBJECTS OF INTEREST ALONG THE ROUTE.

BY

H. F. WALLING.

ILLUSTRATED WITH MAPS.

NEW-YORK:
TAINTOR BROTHERS,
678 BROADWAY.

Entered, according to Act of Congress, in the year 1867, by
TAINTOR BROTHERS & Co.,
In the Clerk's Office of the District Court of the U. S. for the Southern District of New-York.

First Premium Medal and Diploma

Awarded by

American Institute Fair, Oct., 1867.

Also First Premium from every Fair where Exhibited in the East, West, North & South.

HYDRAULIC POWER & HAND
Clothes Washers,

Wringers, Mangles, Air-Current Drying-Rooms, and Domestic Laundry Furniture.

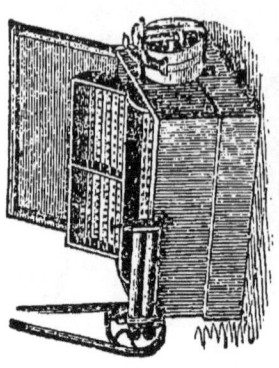

Hydraulic Clothes Washer and Wringer, Steam Power. Price $275 to $500.

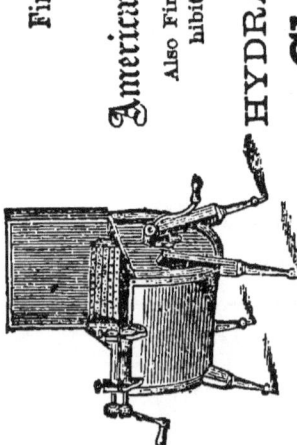

Hydraulic Clothes Washer and Wringer, Hand Power. Price $20 to $50.

Including all the apparatus necessary to supply Housekeepers, Hotels, Public Laundries, Steam Ships, Hospitals, Asylums, Public Institutions, and Private Residences, with a complete set of new and improved Laundry Machinery, with washing capacity of from 1,000 to 5,000 pieces per day; embracing new Inventions superior to anything ever before offered to the Public.

A complete system of rapid cleansing of clothing and family washing of every description. Quilts, Blankets, Laces and articles of delicate texture, without rubbing, pounding, or any friction, by the force of water alone through the fabric; easily operated; not liable to get out of order.

Complete Laundries fitted up by Contract in any part of the country, and of any required capacity.

DESCRIPTIVE PAMPHLETS SENT BY MAIL.

NEW YORK LAUNDRY MANUFACTURING CO.

Office, No. 687 BROADWAY, NEW YORK.

Contents.

Allentown	54
Belvidere	29
Belvidere Delaware Railroad	28
Bethlehem	55
Brick Church	12
Broadway	21
Catasauqua	53
Chatham	14
Coal Regions	25
Columbia	30
Coplay	53
Cranberry Marsh	45
Delaware, Lackawanna, and Western Railroad	30
Delaware Station	30
Delaware Water Gap	30
Denville	15
Dover	17
Drake's Creek	46
Drakesville	17
Dunning	34
Easton	22
East Orange	12
Fairview	45
Freemansburg	56
Furnace	53
Gouldsboro'	34
Greenville	35
Hackettstown	19
Henryville	33
Hickory Run	46
Hoboken	7
Hokendauqua	53
Hutchinson's	28
Laury's	52
Lehigh and Susquehanna Railroad	39
Lehigh Gap	52
Lehighton	51
Lehigh University	56
Lehigh Valley Railroad	44
Lime Ridge	57
Madison	14
Manunka Chunk	29
Martin's Creek	28
Mauch Chunk	47
Methods of Mining Coal	58
Millburn	14
Mill Creek	42
Minooka	14
Montrose	3
Morris and Essex Railroad	15
Morris Plains	15
Morristown	34
Moscow	46
Mud Run	5
Newark	10
Nescopec Station	45
Newport Station	44
Oakland	33
Orange	12
Orange Junction	12
Paradise	33
Parryville	52
Penn Haven Junction	47
Phillipsburg	21
Pittston	40
Pocono Fork	33
Port Morris	18
Port Murray	19
Rockaway	17
Rockdale	52
Rockport	46
Roseville	12
Roxbury	28
Scranton	35-39
Slateford	30
Slatington	52
South Orange	13
South Wilkes Barre	44
Spragueville	33
Spring Brook	40
Stanhope	18
Stewartsville	21
Stony Creek	47
Stroudsburg	32
Sugar Notch	44
Summit Station	14
Switch Back Railway	48
Tannery	46
Tobyhanna	34
Valley Station	13
Warrior Run	44
Washington	19
Waterloo	18
White Haven	45
Wilkes Barre	42
Wyoming Valley	40
Yatesville	43

LOOK AT THESE PRICES

FOR

GENUINE
WALTHAM WATCHES.

SILVER HUNTING WATCHES, ...	$18
GOLD HUNTING WATCHES, 18 carat Cases, . .	$80
GOLD HUNTING WATCHES, Ladies' Size, . .	$70

Every Watch Warranted by Special Certificate from The American Watch Company.

We will send them by Express, with bill to collect on delivery, to all parts of the country, with privilege to the purchaser to examine the Watch before paying; and any Watch that does not perform well can be exchanged, or the money will be cheerfully refunded.

Every one is requested to send for our DESCRIPTIVE PRICE LIST, which explains all the different kinds, gives weight and quality of the case, with prices of each.

Our assortment also comprises every variety of FINE JEWELRY, STERLING SILVER WARE, SILVER-PLATED WARE, and RICH FANCY GOODS.

GORHAM PLATED WARE
At the Manufacturers' Prices.

DIAMOND JEWELRY
ON THE SMALL PROFIT PLAN.

HOWARD & CO.,
Jewelers and Silversmiths,
No. 619 BROADWAY, NEW YORK.

Every one visiting New York is invited to call at our establishment

SEND FOR A PRICE LIST.

Morris and Essex Railroad.

Location, Scenery, Etc.

This important railway traverses the entire State of New-Jersey, from east to west. Commencing at Hoboken, where its terminal freight and passenger stations are directly upon the magnificent harbor of the great metropolis, it passes over the Hackensack marshes to the flourishing manufacturing city of Newark, then crosses the plains of Essex county, thickly studded with suburban villages of unrivaled beauty and prosperity, to the valley at the foot of the beautiful Orange Mountain, along which it passes for some five miles toward the south-west, seeking a passage through the mountain.

A branch of the Rahway having made a breach in the barrier, the railway passes through it at Milburn, and climbs gradually up to the *summit*, on the third of the parallel ridges so remarkably long and continuous, known as the Appalachian system, which extends through the eastern part of the United States, running nearly parallel with the Atlantic for several hundred miles.

From this summit, which commands a most beautiful and extensive prospect toward the south and west, the route continues westward, through an extremely hilly and picturesque country, across the ridges, which are here somewhat broken up, to Waterloo, running for many miles near the route of the *Morris Canal*. This section is one of the most important iron-mining and smelting regions in the country.

The railroad now enters the head of the *Shenandoah Valley*, so called, being, in fact, between two of the several parallel ridges which extend, with various breaks and curious zigzags, through Pennsylvania, Maryland, and Virginia. The local names of these ridges are, *Schooley's Mountain*, on the south-east side of the valley, and *Pohatcong Mountain*, on the north-west. Whether the particular valley occupied by the Shenandoah River in Virginia can be continuously traced to this, among these irregularities, is perhaps of little consequence. It is in the same great series, and substantially the same valley. The same rich, fertile farming lands are seen, with their inclosing hills, arable to their summits.

At Washington the route passes through a gap in the Pohatcong Mountain, and, for the remainder of the distance, runs in the valley between it and the hills to the north-west, the Pohatcong Creek and the Morris Canal being in the same valley. Similar beautiful fertile pastoral scenery continues, however, in this valley to that found on the other side of the Pohatcong.

At Phillipsburg we come to the Delaware River, the boundary between New-Jersey and Pennsylvania, across which a magnificent iron bridge has been built, to connect with the railways converging at Easton.

HISTORY.

The *Morris and Essex* Railroad Company was chartered in 1835, with authority to construct a road from Newark to the Delaware River, opposite Easton. The construction was commenced in the fall of 1835, and the road opened to Morristown, 23 miles, in 1837; to Dover, 11 miles further, in 1848; to Hackettstown, 19 miles further, in January, 1854; and to Easton, in November, 1865. A second track is being laid on the entire route, and is completed to Morristown. In 1857, a charter was obtained for an extension from Newark to Hoboken, which was completed in 1863, passing through the Bergen Tunnel, nearly a mile in length. This tunnel, however, is the property of the Long Dock Company, of which the stock is owned by the Erie Railway Company.

BRANCHES AND CONNECTIONS.

The *Newark and Bloomfield Railroad*, of which more than half the stock is owned by the Morris and Essex Railroad Company, extends, from its junction with the latter railroad in the western part of Newark, through a corner of the town of East-Orange and the village of Bloomfield, to the village of Mont Clair, in the western part of the town of Bloomfield, and is six miles long. It is in contemplation to extend this road to Boonton, thus making a more direct and favorable route to Easton.

From Newark the trains of the *New-Jersey Railroad* run to New-Brunswick, connecting at that point with the *Camden and Amboy* for Trenton, Philadelphia, and all points south.

From *Denville* a branch extends five miles to *Boonton*, an important iron manufacturing place.

At *Waterloo* is the junction of the *Sussex Railroad*, extending to Newton, in Sussex county, 12 miles, through a rich iron-mining country. Important accessions to the freight business of the main road are derived from this branch in the way of transporting ores, etc.

At Washington the *Delaware, Lackawanna, and Western Railroad* crosses the Morris and Essex, bringing to it an immense quantity of coal freight and no insignificant amount of passenger travel, especially in the summer months.

These branches augment the large local business which a road traversing the centre of a great State like New-Jersey, and across her most active mining and manufacturing region, as well as through some of her most fertile and productive agricultural valleys, can not fail to secure. But in addition to this, the Morris and Essex Railroad has a vast present and prospective importance, as a great main thoroughfare between the metropolis of the country and the great States west of New-Jersey, including Pennsylvania, the great coal and iron State, with whose mines, furnaces, and forges connection is made by the three great railroads converging at Easton, namely, the Belvidere Delaware, extending both ways up and down the Delaware River, from Trenton to Belvidere, the Lehigh Valley Railroad, and the Lehigh Coal and Navigation Company's Railroad, the two latter connecting with the great anthracite coal business of Lackawanna, Wyoming, Lehigh, Mahanoy and Schuylkill, and, through their connections, with all the great iron-mining and manufacturing regions of the State.

STATISTICS.

Capital stock	$3,500,000
Funded debt	5,516,950
Cost of road, including buildings, etc.	6,973,931
Cost of engines	1,153,329
Cost of cars	1,027,782
Locomotives burning wood	25
Locomotives burning anthracite coal	18
Locomotives burning bituminous coal	3
Total locomotives	46
Passenger cars	62
Baggage and mail cars	9
Cabooses	11
Freight cars	284
Iron and ore cars	100
Coal cars (eight-wheel)	400

During the year 1866, 1,066,179 passengers were transported over the road, exclusive of commuters and those who ride free.

Dividends to the amount of seven per cent on the capital stock were paid during the year.

FUTURE PROSPECTS.

This railroad is clearly destined to become, and that before many years, one of the most important thoroughfares between New-York City and the great interior and Western States. The utmost capacities of all the railroads tending in that direction must ere long, in the natural course of events, be most fully employed in transacting the constantly and rapidly increasing business between the vast continent and its metropolis.

The internal improvements and local wealth of Northern New-Jersey, while they are vastly increased by the facilities afforded by this avenue of traffic, will in turn react favorably upon the prosperity of the railroad.

Travelers desiring to go west *via* the Morris and Essex Railroad cross from New-York to Hoboken by *either* of the two ferries. That from the foot of Barclay street accommodates the lower portion of the city, while, for those living above Canal street, the Christopher street ferry is most convenient, both landing at the same place in Hoboken. The passenger station is on the left of the ferry landing, in Hoboken, at the south-eastern extremity of that city.

HOBOKEN.
Hoboken, Hudson Co., N. J.
2 *m. fr. N. Y.   Fr. Easton,* **83**.

This suburban city is a convenient place of resort and recreation for the citizens of New-York, containing many handsome residences, overlooking the North River, and various objects of interest to the traveler.

Here is the well-known and delightful park, called the "*Elysian Fields,*" stretching to the north along the riverbank for nearly a mile, shaded with grand old English elms and forest-trees, that line the winding paths, and remind one of the trees in which, according to Virgil, "the dreams have their abode." Here frequent cricket

NEW YORK TO MORRISTOWN.

and base-ball matches attract thousands of spectators, and multitudes from the metropolis seek fresh air and healthful recreation. These "Elysian Fields" are owned by Mr. Stevens, whose residence is seen to the north, upon the height of Castle Point, and who admits the public to this shady retreat free of charge. Near the shore is a structure of heavy timbers, containing a huge cannon, which was planted there by Mr. Stevens for the purpose of testing the plates of his great iron-clad ram, upon the construction of which he has been engaged for many years, and which still remains unfinished.

This city contains eleven churches, a bank, a savings institution, two newspaper offices, numerous hotels, a costly club-house, and many large stores and storehouses.

Two lines of European steamers depart from this port, namely, the "North-German Lloyd's" and the "Hamburg-American Packet" Companies. Their piers are a short distance north of the ferry. South are the extensive coal-yards of the Morris and Essex Railroad, and the docks of numerous steam and sailing vessels.

Passing out from the station-house, we soon leave the limits of Hoboken, and ride along the northern boundary of Jersey City, over a tract which was formerly a low marsh, but which has now been reclaimed and covered with dwellings. Turning a sharp curve to the south and another to the west, we are brought for a few moments to a stand-still at the mouth of the BERGEN TUNNEL, cut through the solid trap-rock of Bergen Heights, a distance of more than three quarters of a mile.

These heights form the southern extremity of those precipitous rocky cliffs which extend for many miles along the west bank of the Hudson River, and are known as the *Palisades*.

Entering the tunnel, we seem to be at once hurried from day to night, the total darkness only being relieved as we pass the occasional lights that faintly illumine the subterranean gloom.

Emerging from this *tunnel*, we cross the Hackensack River, and ride for three or four miles over a level, marshy tract waving with tall grass, resembling a prairie, through which the Hackensack winds its sluggish and tortuous way. Across this marsh, along beside the turnpike to Hudson City, extends the Jersey City Aqueduct, from the Passaic River to a reservoir upon Bergen Heights. Also, nearly parallel, for about two miles, with the *Morris and Essex Railroad*, the *New-Jersey* Railway runs, forming a part of the route between New-York and Philadelphia. A company has recently been formed, with a capital of thirty millions, for the purpose of reclaiming these meadows, and rendering them available for cultivation and building purposes.

SNAKE HILL, a remarkable wooded eminence, rises abruptly out of this marsh, one mile north of the railroad. Upon it stands the Hudson County Almshouse, in full view from the cars. Beyond these marshes, which are some four miles wide, the land rises by a gentle slope, covered with villages, with mountains in the distance bounding the vision.

The *Passaic* River now comes in sight on the left, and the city of

NEWARK.

Newark, Essex County, N. J.
10 *m. fr. N. Y. Fr. Easton,* **75**.
HOTEL—*Newark House.*

LOCATION AND APPEARANCE.

The city of Newark, the largest in the State, and the tenth city of the Union, having a population of nearly 100,000, is situated on the right bank of the Passaic River, four miles from its entrance into Newark Bay, chiefly on an elevated plain, terminated on the west by a ridge of land, extending from its northern to its southern extremity. It is regularly and handsomely laid out, with wide, straight streets, intersecting at right angles, and everywhere shaded with a profusion of magnificent elms, which line both sides of its streets in unbroken ranks. *Broad* street is the principal business thoroughfare, 120 feet in breadth, and extends through the entire length of the city, dividing it into two nearly equal parts. Crossing Broad street near its centre, is Market street, another important avenue of trade. Above Market street, and bordering on Broad, are two beautiful public squares, called "Washington" and "Military" Parks, each adorned with a profusion of shade-trees. In the lower part of the city is the "South Park," younger than the other two, and containing only trees of recent growth.

PUBLIC BUILDINGS.

Among its *public buildings* are the *Court-House*, a large and handsome brown stone edifice, in the Egyptian style of architecture, at the intersection of Market and High streets. The building of the Library Association, containing a library of over 12,000 volumes, is one of the finest in the city. Besides apartments for the library, it contains a large hall for public lectures and concerts. The Custom-House, Post-Office, and City Hall will also attract attention. The Newark Academy is a fine brick building, situated on the most elegant part of High street, and is surrounded by pleasant grounds, where an extended view is obtained of the Passaic Valley. The city of Newark contains seventy-five churches, lifting their spires skyward, and deserves the cognomen of "The City of Churches" equally with its sister city, Brooklyn. Among the most prominent are the Presbyterian on High street, the Methodist on Church street, the Episcopal on Broad street, and the St. James's Cathedral. The building occupied by the Mutual Benefit Life Insurance Company is one of the finest in the State.

MANUFACTURES.

Newark owes its rapid growth chiefly to its extensive manufactories, numbering nearly eight hundred, and causing it to rank the third city of the Union in manufacturing importance. The amount of capital employed in these pursuits is between ten and eleven millions of dollars, while the value of manufactured articles aggregates more than twenty-one millions annually.

While crossing the Passaic River, before reaching the station, *Fagin's flour mill* rises prominently in view, to the south on the river bank. The building is immense, the largest establishment of the kind, probably, in the world, being 156 feet or twelve stories high, and 85 feet wide by 150 feet long. It is not only a monster grain elevator, but also a "huge hive of industry," turning out 2000 barrels of flour daily. The chimney at its side is 175 feet high. In the construction of this mill a million and a half of brick were used, its first story being built of brown stone, laid upon a foundation of solid granite piers; and the entire structure is so compactly framed together that it is said the outer walls might be torn away, while every floor was laden with grain, and still the building would stand as firmly as a rock. There are a little over two *acres* of floors in the mill, and, were it used for storage, it would hold 760,000 bushels of grain. The entire machinery is driven by two engines of 600 horse-power.

Connected with the establishment is a cooper-shop which can easily manufacture 2000 barrels daily, and is capable of holding 30,000.

The firm of Fagin & Co. have erected this mill at Newark on account of the unobstructed facilities for navigation which the Passaic River possesses over the crowded harbor of New-York. The view from its cupola is very extended.

A little above it and nearer the railroad bridge is Ballantine's huge *Brewery*, where thousands of barrels of ale are manufactured annually. North of the railroad bridge are the factories of the *Clark Thread Company*, one of the largest thread works in the country, giving employment to 750 girls, and the Rankin Mills.

Besides these there are in Newark establishments for the production of India-rubber goods, carriages, paper, machinery, castings, boots and shoes, etc. In the manufacture of *jewelry* this city is perhaps not surpassed by any in the United States, while in all the various branches of industry it presents a most busy and prosperous appearance.

Here are some very celebrated *brown stone quarries*, which furnish great quantities of building material for New-York stores and residences, as well as for home consumption. In its commerce Newark is limited chiefly to the coasting trade, the Passaic River being navigable only for vessels of light draught.

OBJECTS OF INTEREST.

In the vicinity of *Newark* are many pleasant drives and walks. The shore of the Passaic River is lined with many beautiful villas, and elegant residences, which are seldom surpassed in the taste and costliness of their ornamentation. Among the more interesting of these is the "Kearny Place," the residence of the late General Kearny, one of the nation's gallant defenders during the late war. It stands in a forest, and is built in the French style of architecture. On the opposite shore from the Kearny Place stands the ancient house, immortalized by Washington Irving in the *Salmagundi*, under the title of "*Cockloft Hall.*" Just beyond are the "*Cedars*," the former home of Henry William Herbert, known in literary circles as "*Frank Forrester.*" Here he lived an almost hermit life devoted to literature and dissipation, and here died. *Mount Pleasant Cemetery*, north of the city, embraces thirty-five acres of pleasantly undulating grounds, with smooth, winding avenues, and a deluge of flowers that load the air with a grateful perfume.

HISTORY, ETC.

Newark was settled in 1666 by a

company of Puritan families from New-Haven and adjoining colonies, the influence of whose character in moulding the future of the town is witnessed at the present day in the marked morality and respect for religious observances that distinguish this city above others.

At present, it is true, it has a large foreign population, and is the see of a Roman Catholic Bishop, yet its small police force and general good order is a standing testimonial of its character.

RAILWAY CONNECTIONS, ETC.

The Newark and Bloomfield Railway connects with the pleasant suburban towns of Roseville, Bloomfield, and Mont Clair, while horse railroads run to Belleville, Clinton, Orange, and other adjoining places. The Morris Canal passes through the city, and a fine passenger steamboat plies daily to and from New-York. A railroad to Paterson is now being constructed.

We now enter the fine farming country of New-Jersey, with the Orange Hills in view on the right, and pass up, for a short distance, a steep ascending grade of 140 feet to the mile.

ROSEVILLE.

Newark, Essex Co., N. J.
11 *m. fr. N. Y. Fr. Easton,* **75.**

This station is in the western part of the city of Newark, and is at the junction of the Morris and Essex with the Newark and Bloomfield Railroad, extending through Bloomfield to Mont Clair.

The village of BLOOMFIELD contains many beautiful summer residences of New-York business men, and is healthful and pleasant. It is some two miles in length, and contains several churches and seminaries. In its vicinity are manufactories of cotton and woolen goods and paper.

MONT CLAIR is another handsome and flourishing suburban village in the western part of the town of Bloomfield, just under the mountain.

EAST-ORANGE,

Orange, Essex Co., N. J.,
12 *m. fr. N. Y. Fr. Easton,* **74,**

Is a pleasant village, containing some handsome suburban residences and rich farms. A new church, recently erected here, is seen on the left, near the station. The main street runs nearly north and south.

ORANGE JUNCTION,

Orange, Essex Co., N. J.,
12¼ *m. fr. N. Y. Fr. Easton,* **73¼,**

Receives its name from its being the junction of the Morris and Essex Railroad with the Newark Horse Railway. A new depot has recently been built here, to accommodate the residents in the east part of Orange.

BRICK CHURCH.

Orange, Essex Co., N. J.
13 *m. fr. N. Y. Fr. Easton* **73.**

Named from a church near this station, which is built of brick. A beautiful street here runs nearly parallel with the track, a little distance to the north of it, lined with pleasant residences.

Harrison street, which is crossed by the railroad a little west of the station, is one of the principal streets of the town of Orange, and is more than a mile in length.

ORANGE.

Orange, Essex Co., N. J.
14 *m. fr. N. Y. Fr. Easton,* **72.**

Orange has become noted as one of

the finest suburban towns in the environs of New-York.

The salubrity of its climate, the beautiful scenery in its vicinity, and the facility of access to the city, have made it a favorite location for men of wealth and elegant tastes, wishing to retire from the bustle and confusion of the city.

Many elegant and costly residences have been erected here, and the place is rapidly growing in importance.

Within a few years the original town of Orange has been subdivided into several smaller ones, so that we now have East-Orange, West-Orange, and South-Orange, besides Orange proper.

WEST-ORANGE, immediately adjoining Orange on the west, includes a portion of Orange Mountain and the well-known *Lewellyn Park*. Here the rugged mountain-side has been converted by the taste and skill of Mr. L. S. Haskell, the originator of the project, into a series of beautiful villa sites, peculiarly adapted for landscape gardening, and for artistic architectural effects in the erection of suburban residences.

Winding avenues, finely shaded with forest-trees and shrubbery, lead from the main entrance to all the different tracts into which it is subdivided, and portions of it, especially adapted for that purpose by their wild and romantic beauty, are laid out as common parks for the benefit of all the residents. The view from *Eagle Rock*, the most elevated and prominent point in the park, is indescribably grand and beautiful. From this and numerous other points in the park, New-York City, Brooklyn, the Bay, Staten Island, etc., are distinctly visible.

VALLEY STATION.
Orange, Essex Co., N. J.
15 *m. fr. N. Y. Fr. Easton,* **71.**

Here are extensive felt hat manufactories. More hats are made in this vicinity than in any other part of the country. A fine stone church is being erected here, on the hill east of the railroad. We now pass along the hillside, overlooking a beautiful valley and the slopes of the Orange Mountain on the west.

MONTROSE.
South Orange, Essex Co., N. J.
15¼ *m. fr. N. Y. Fr. Easton,* **70¾.**

Here quite a large tract has been purchased and laid out in lots, presenting many delightful building sites to those desiring a country location.

A new depot has recently been erected at this point.

SOUTH-ORANGE,
South Orange, Essex Co., N. J.
16 *m. fr. N. Y. Fr. Easton,* **70,**

Is one of the most delightful portions of Essex county. Its location is in the valley and on the slopes lying between First or Orange Mountain on the west, and a range of low hills on the east, and is the summer residence of numbers of men doing business in New-York. Along the mountain-side are many beautiful suburban villas and country-seats, embowered among trees, while their elevated site affords a magnificent view to the eastward of this entire region, extending many miles. The cities of New-York and Brooklyn, Newark, Elizabeth, and Rahway can be distinctly seen from Orange Mountain, in a clear day, while the numerous villages and rich landscape lying between form a scene of surpassing beauty.

Seton Hall, a Roman Catholic college, is pleasantly situated, a half mile east of the railroad, on the carriage-road to Newark.

MILLBURN.

Millburn, Essex Co., N. J.
20 *m. fr. N. Y. Fr. Easton,* **66.**

Millburn is a pleasant village, on the left of the railroad, containing two churches and some fine residences. There are also several hat manufactories and an extensive manufactory of paper. We here pass around the extremity of the Orange Mountain, which breaks off abruptly into what are called the " Short Hills." The grade here ascends about 80 feet to the mile to the summit, and the view toward the south, as we pass on, is extensive and beautiful.

SUMMIT STATION.

New-Providence, Union Co., N. J.
23 *m. fr. N. Y. Fr. Easton,* **63.**

This station, as its name indicates, is on the top of the mountain, over which the railroad here passes. Looking toward the left or eastward, we obtain a view of Elizabeth in the distance, with Springfield and other villages lying between, and a fertile country, dotted with neat farm-houses. Here, on the *left,* is a small village, with a church, several stores, and a number of summer residences.

The Summit House, a large hotel, is also beautifully situated near the depot. The view westward is very extended. *Boonton,* distinguished for its iron furnaces and manufactories, is seen far off upon the mountains, and Chat-ham, a few miles distant. After leaving the station we pass, on a descending grade, through a wooded and hilly country, often winding from toward the north and south by sharp curves. Again we cross the Passaic, with the little village of Stanley, or South-Chatham, on the west, where there are several large paper-mills, and the manufacture of felt roofing is extensively carried on. The wooded elevation west of it is called " Long Hill."

CHATHAM,

Chatham, Morris Co., N. J.,
25 *m. fr. N. Y. Fr. Easton,* **60,**

Is a handsome village, in a rolling country, on the Passaic River. It contains a church, several stores, and an academy. There are many fine farms in the township. Land in this vicinity has become quite valuable, a number of the most desirable localities having been secured for summer residences by gentlemen from the city.

MADISON,

Chatham, Morris Co., N. J.,
28 *m. fr. N. Y. Fr. Easton,* **57,**

Formerly called "*Bottle Hill,*" contains several stores and churches, and a manufactory of screws. It is pleasantly located in a fertile region, the land in some localities selling at $1000 and upward per acre. Many New-York business men own dwellings here. *Daniel Drew,* of New-York, has bought 200 acres of land in Madison, at a cost of $150,000, and given it to the Methodists for the purpose of establishing a theological seminary, and has offered a much larger sum to insure its success.

Leaving this station, Boonton again

MORRISTOWN,

Morristown, Morris Co., N. J.,
32 *m. fr. N. Y. Fr. Easton,* **53,**

comes in nearer view as we overlook the valley.

Is the capital of Morris county, on the Whippany River. It is situated on a table-land inclosed by ranges of hills, and presents a neat and attractive appearance. It has a handsome court-house, eight churches, two banks, an academy, and several private schools, with many fine residences. In the centre is a handsome public square, on which are erected many of the stores and public buildings. It is the principal market for the rich and highly productive agricultural region that surrounds it, and has manufactories of paper, iron, etc.

General Washington had his head-quarters here during the encampment of the army in this vicinity in the winters of 1776 and 1779. The house then occupied by him can be seen just before arriving at the depot, on the right of the track, beyond the meadow, which extends from the front of the house to the railroad. It was built in 1774, and contains a number of articles of furniture which were then used by him. "Fort Nonsense" is an elevated piece of ground just back of the Court-House, on which some slight evidences of fortifications may still be traced. Upon the old camping-ground of the army the foundations of many of the chimneys erected by the troops may be seen, running in parallel rows, and terminating on what is called *Fort Hill*, south of the village, where probably artillery was located.

At Baskingridge, about six miles south-west of Morristown, stands the house in which Major-General Charles Lee was captured, while loitering on his way to join Washington, in December, 1776. About a mile eastward of Baskingridge, a mansion erected by Earl Sterling soon after his marriage with the daughter of Philip Livingston is still standing.

Several days may be passed by a traveler very pleasantly at Morristown in visiting these historic localities. The village has a number of good hotels, with a population of about four thousand. After leaving here, we run nearly due north through a hilly and rough tract for several miles.

MORRIS PLAINS,

Morristown, Morris Co., N. J.,
34 *m. fr. N. Y. Fr. Easton,* **51,**

Is a small station bordering on the town of Hanover, with but a few houses.

DENVILLE.

Rockaway, Morris Co., N. J.
39 *m. fr. N. Y. Fr. Easton,* **46.**

Here is a hotel and small village. Mountains and wooded hills are seen on every side as we ride onward, and we again approach quite near to the Morris Canal, which from Newark runs north to Paterson, thence west through Boonton to this place, and from here pursues a course nearly parallel with the railroad as far as Easton. A branch railroad connects this place with Boonton, five miles north-east.

BOONTON is situated in one of the most mountainous sections of Morris county, on the Rockaway River, surrounded by high hills and rocky ascents, upon which much of the village is built.

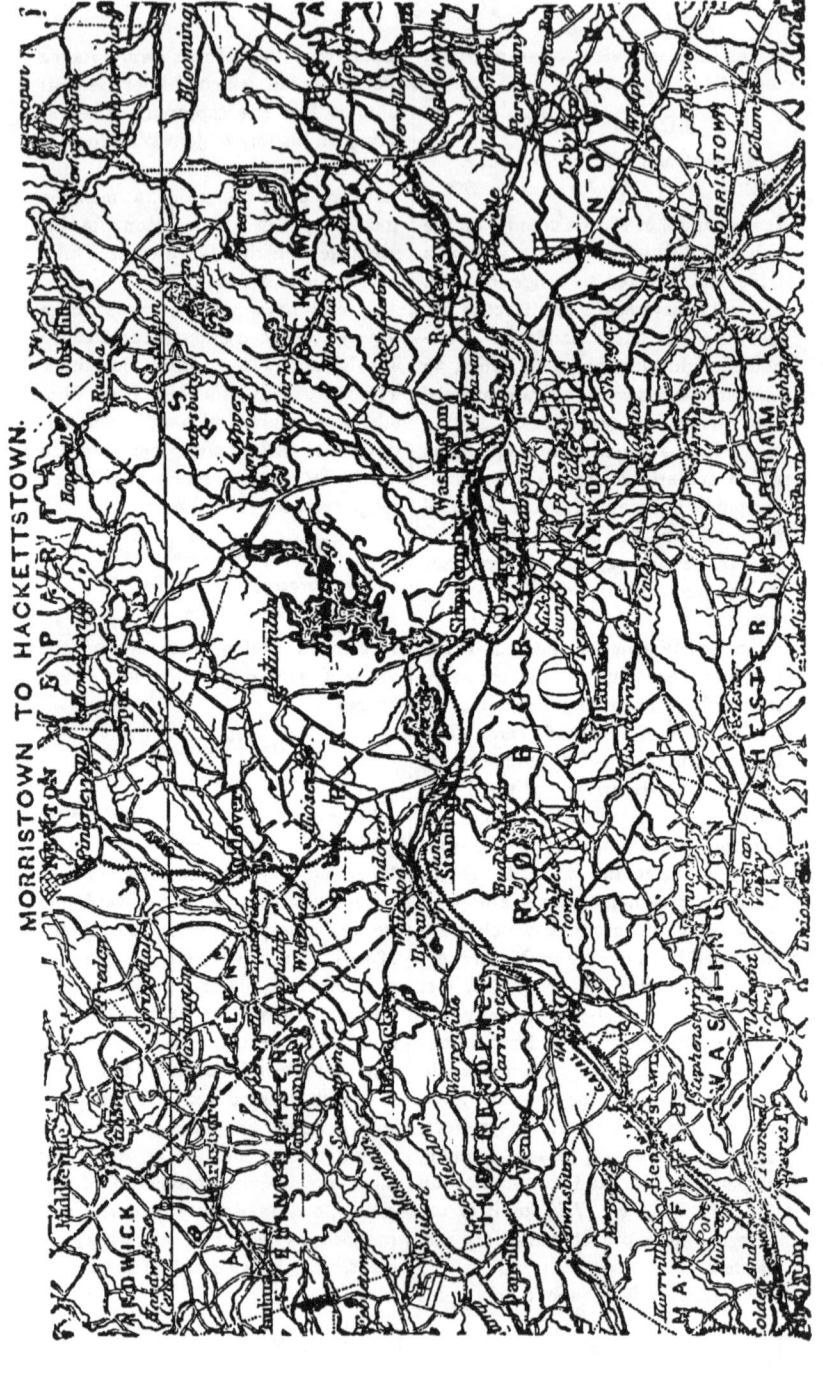

It is distinguished for its extensive *iron works*, which consist of a blast-furnace, a large rolling-mill, and a nail factory, the whole forming one of the most complete establishments of the kind in the country.

The iron used here is principally obtained from the Mount Hope and Hibernia Mines, situated a few miles west, in the adjoining township of Rockaway. The Morris Canal and the new branch railroad to Denville afford valuable facilities both for the transportation of ore and of the manufactured products.

The village contains two or three churches, several stores, two hotels, and some pleasant residences. Here are several inclined planes on the Morris Canal, by means of which boats are drawn from one level to another over the hills.

The elevated position of Boonton renders it visible for many miles around, and the prospect from its vicinity is varied and extensive.

ROCKAWAY.

Rockaway, Morris Co., N. J.
41 *m. fr. N. Y. Fr. Easton,* **44.**

Rockaway, on the Rockaway River, is one of the most important towns in the State, being situated in its richest iron mining region, and having extensive manufactories of this metal. Here are large rolling-mills, several forges and foundries, and steel furnaces. Railroad tracks lead from this station back into the mines, bringing down the ore to the furnaces and to the railroad. We now follow for a time the right bank of the Rockaway River, and soon reach

DOVER.

Randolph, Morris Co., N. J.
44 *m. fr. N. Y. Fr. Easton,* **41.**

Dover, near the centre of Morris county, and in the midst of a rich mining region, is next to Morristown in importance. It is upon the Rockaway River and the Morris Canal. It contains several manufactories of iron and steel, with their furnaces, foundries, rolling-mills, etc., also several spike factories. The village contains a church, bank, and several stores. The "*Jolly House*" will do its best to make all visitors to this locality good-natured.

Leaving Dover, we cross the Morris Canal and pass through a wooded region, frequently crossing and recrossing the Rockaway River amid numerous romantic hills, and passing the junction of the *Mount Hope Railroad* on the right, leading to the Mount Hope Mines on the mountains, some four miles north of the main road. These mines are owned by the Lackawanna Iron and Coal Company, who mine over 10,000 tons per annum. The Thomas Iron Company and the Glendon Iron Company also have extensive mines near this road.

DRAKESVILLE.

Roxbury, Morris Co., N. J.
49 *m. fr. N. Y. Fr. Easton,* **33.**

Lake Hopatcong is four miles distant from this station, on a mountain to the north. This lake is nine miles long and about four wide, and is a popular summer resort. In its vicinity are five hotels, which accommodate large numbers of guests. Two small steamboats ply over its waters, which abound with fish. It is one of the feeders of the

Morris Canal, and is remarkable as having no visible inlet. The village of Drakesville is a mile and a half southeast from the depot. Stages are, however, in waiting to convey passengers to it and to the lake houses.

PORT MORRIS,
Roxbury, Morris Co., N. J.,
51 *m. fr. N. Y. Fr. Easton,* **34,**

Also called Shipping Port, being the point where coal is transhipped from the canal to the railroad. There are several inclined planes along the canal in this vicinity, where the boats are transferred from one level to another, in getting over the summit formed by the ridge known on the south-west as Schooley's Mountain and on the northeast as Brookland Mountain. These two mountains, having the convenient gap between through which the canal and railroad find passage, form a part of the great Appalachian range of mountains extending many hundred miles along the eastern part of the United States.

Stationary engines are used for hoisting the boats up these planes, but on the downward progress they descend by their own weight. The southern extremity of Lake Hopatcong approaches quite near this station, and its water is drawn into Brookland Pond, which lies a little north of the railroad, and forms a part of the canal for some distance near Stanhope.

The Ogden Mine Railroad is being extended to connect with the railroad at this place. It now runs from the mines to the canal at Brookland Pond, ten miles. Five miles more are to be built to reach the Morris and Essex Railroad at Port Morris.

STANHOPE,
Roxbury, Morris Co., N. J.,
53 *m. fr. N. Y. Fr. Easton,* **31,**

On the *Musconetcong* River, which has its source in Lake *Hopatcong*. It contains a large iron furnace, which can be seen on the right, with a branch track leading to it, and about sixty dwellings. About three miles from this station to the north is *Lake Senecawana*, sometimes called *Budd's Lake*, a beautiful sheet of water five miles long and two wide, on the east side of which there is a fine *hotel*, which has become a popular summer resort. Omnibuses run from the depot to the Lake House.

WATERLOO.
Roxbury, Morris Co., N. J.
56 *m fr. N. Y. Fr. Easton,* **29.**

Waterloo is a small village on the Musconetcong River, with a few houses. Pohatcong Mountain, nearly on the north-west, affords a fine view of the surrounding country. Here the Morris and Essex Railroad connects with the Sussex Railroad, running to Newton, ten miles distant.

NEWTON, the terminus of the Sussex Railroad, is a thriving borough, and capital of Sussex county. It is pleasantly situated on the Paulinskill Creek, upon an undulating site, bounded on the west by a range of hills that extend north and south through the entire length of the county, while on the east extended meadows stretch northward along the Paulinskill. It is handsomely laid out, and contains the county courthouse and jail, five churches, a bank, several good schools, and a public library. Here are also two large iron foundries. The population of Newton is about 3500. Within the township are the "Andover" and "Tar" iron mines. A branch railroad from the former connects with the Sussex Railroad, and, through it, with the Morris and Essex Railway.

HACKETTSTOWN,

Hackettstown, Warren Co., N. J.
62 *m. fr. N. Y. Fr. Easton,* **23**.
HOTELS—*American* and *Warren Houses.*

Is a thriving borough on the *Musconetcong* River, near the Morris Canal, with a population of 2000. It was incorporated in 1852, and contains a number of churches and stores, a bank, and an academy, and has also extensive flouring-mills. Its situation is in the midst of a delightful and fertile agricultural valley, of limestone formation, which yields a rich return to the farmer. The town is in full view on the left as we approach the station.

SCHOOLEY'S MOUNTAIN, two and a half miles distant, is a celebrated watering-place. This mountain has an elevation of 1200 feet above the sea. *Mineral Springs*, containing muriate of soda, of lime, and of magnesia, sulphate of lime, carbonate of magnesia, and carbonated oxide of iron, are found near its summit. Several hotels and private boarding-houses have been erected here for the accommodation of visitors, who resort here to drink the waters, and enjoy the pure air and mountain scenery. Omnibuses are always at the station to convey passengers to these mountain hotels, and also through the village. The sharp peak rising abruptly west of the station is called *Malvern Hill*, from which Easton can be seen on a clear day. The Morris Canal passes near its base. The large building upon the bank of the canal is a Lager-Bier Brewery. We have now entered what is called the head of the Shenandoah Valley, being formed by similar ridges to that of the Shenandoah Valley in Virginia, and indeed forming a part of the same Appalachian range. The ridge on the south-east is Schooley's Mountain, that on the north-west Pohatcong Mountain. The Musconetcong River runs in this valley to its junction with the Delaware, four or five miles below Easton.

PORT MURRAY,

Washington, Warren Co., N. J.,
68 *m. fr. N. Y. Fr. Easton,* **17**,

A small way station on the north-west side of the valley near Pohatcong Mountain. It is likewise a station on the canal, and has a hotel and one or two stores. There is near by a fine quarry of handsome, light-colored granite, which is used for building purposes. This is a favorite locality for sportsmen; quail and woodcock abound, while nearly all the streams contain trout.

WASHINGTON.

Washington, Warren Co., N. J.
72 *m. fr. N. Y. Fr. Easton,* **14**.
HOTEL—The *Washington House.*

The Delaware, Lackawanna, and Western Railroad here intersects the Morris and Essex, and passengers for the Lackawanna and Wyoming coal regions, Scranton, the Delaware Water-Gap, etc., change cars here.

Both these railroads here find their way through a wide gap in the Pohatcong Mountain. While the former winds its way across the ridges toward the north-west, the latter and the Morris Canal continue in a south-westerly

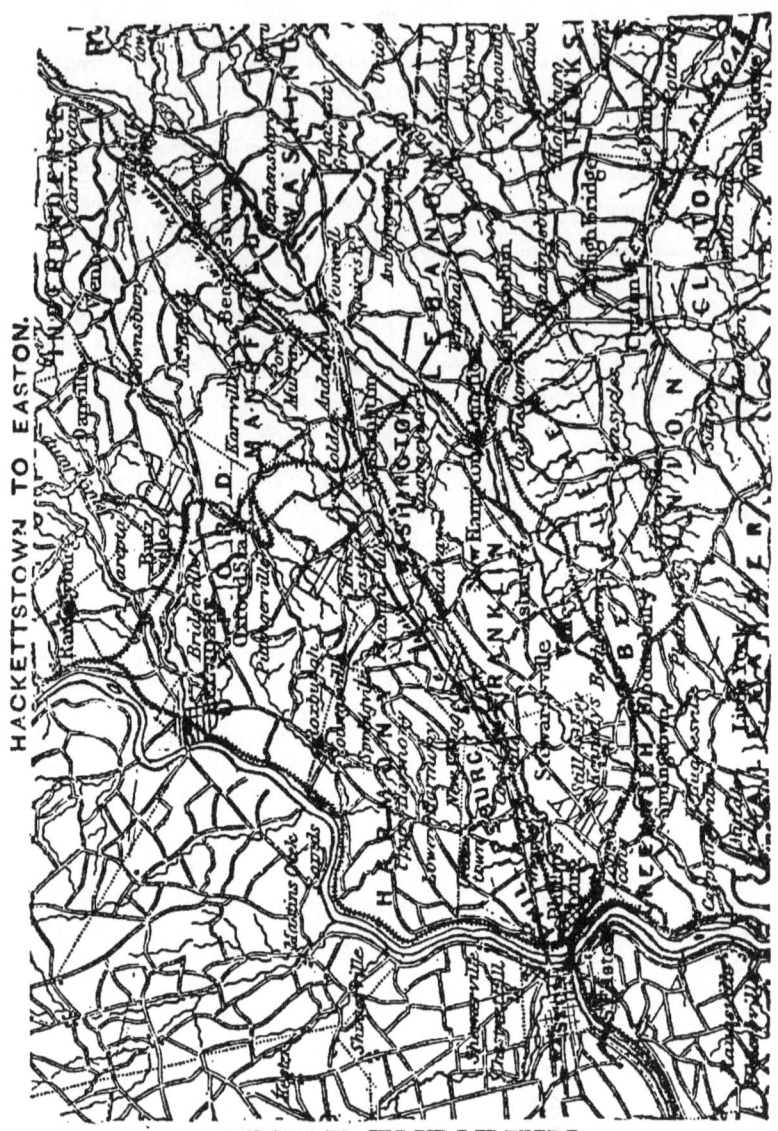

GREAT EMPORIUM
FOR
STEREOSCOPES AND VIEWS
OF ALL PARTS OF THE WORLD,
Photographic Albums, and Photographic Materials,
E. & H. T. ANTHONY & CO.,
501 BROADWAY, New York, St. Nicholas Block.

CHROMOS.

These beautiful pictures, that *cannot be distinguished from the finest Oil Paintings*, at one-tenth their cost, we import largely from Paris, London, Berlin, Vienna, and Rome, and supply the trade at the lowest rates.

direction, along the valley formed by the Pohatcong on the south-east and Scott Mountain on the north-west.

Washington is a beautiful village of 1500 inhabitants. It has several large stores, a large Masonic hall, two churches, an academy, and many handsome residences. It is a thriving business place. The Delaware, Lackawanna, and Western Railroad Company here transship large quantities of coal to the canal. The amount so transshipped during the last year was 200,000 tons. The hills on the south contain iron ore, while the smooth, rolling country on the north is extremely fertile, producing rich harvests of grass and cereals. A mile below is a large flour-mill and brick-yard.

BROADWAY,

Franklin, Warren Co., N. J.,
77 *m. fr. N. Y. Fr. Easton,* **9,**

Is a small country village, about three quarters of a mile north of the station, on Pohatcong Creek. It contains a church and store, with about twenty dwellings. Considerable grain is forwarded from this vicinity.

STEWARTSVILLE,

Greenwich, Warren Co., N. J.,
71 *m. fr. N. Y. Fr. Easton,* **5,**

Is situated on Merritt's Brook, a branch of Pohatcong Creek. It is an old-fashioned, inland town, with a population of about five hundred, having considerable wealth, most of its citizens being thriving farmers. There is an extensive tannery here, which, in the perfection and variety of its machinery, is said to be second to none in the State; also a large brick-yard. It has also three churches, several stores, and an academy. The railroad crosses the Morris Canal at this place. Beyond Stewartsville we pass through a deep cut in the earth and rock, seventy feet deep, in excavating which a year and a half was occupied.

PHILLIPSBURG.

Phillipsburg, Warren Co., N. J.
83 *m. fr. N. Y. Fr. Easton,* **1.**
HOTELS—*Bennet's* and *Reese's.*

An incorporated borough, situated on the left bank of the Delaware River, opposite Easton, in Pennsylvania. Its site is on a high elevation, somewhat rocky and uneven in surface, yet it has many pleasant cottages and villas, and considerable wealth. It is an important manufacturing town, having twelve large establishments, where iron in some form is the product.

Among these are the "Trenton Iron Company's Furnace;" a nut manufactory; the Warren Foundry and Machine Company's Works, for the manufacture of gas and water-pipes; Reese, Merrick & Co.'s manufactory of mowing-machines and agricultural implements; the Delaware Rolling-Mill; Delaware Bolt Factory; Lake, Bearder & Co.'s stove works; Wilhelm Wagner & Co.'s sheet-iron manufactory, the product of which is said to be equal in quality to that of any manufactory in the United States. There are four churches in this borough. Three bridges cross the Delaware at this place—two of wood, for the Lehigh Valley Railroad, and a new iron one, recently built, for the Morris and Essex Railroad. Phillipsburg is the residence of General Heckman, who distinguished himself in the late war for the maintenance of the Union.

Here connection is made with the Belvidere Delaware Railroad, the *Lehigh Valley Railroad*, and the *Lehigh Coal and Navigation Company's Railroad*.

A connection is also contemplated with the *East Pennsylvania Railroad* at Allentown, by building a new railroad from Easton to that place. The East Pennsylvania Railroad is now controlled by the Reading Railroad Company, and by this means an outlet will be afforded for the great Schuylkill and ·Mahanoy Coal Regions directly to New-York, *via* Pottsville and Tamaqua.

The interests of the Lehigh coal region are intimately connected with those of the two railroads now existing between Easton and Allentown, and they are not at present disposed to allow the coal of the other regions to pass over their road, to compete with theirs in the New-York market.

EASTON.

Easton, Northampton Co., Pa.
86 m. fr. N. Y.

HOTELS—The *American* and *Franklin Houses*.

SITE.

This town, one of the oldest in the State, is situated at the junction of the Delaware, Lehigh, and Bushkill Rivers, in part upon the *débris* which their waters have washed down and lodged in this situation. So limited, however, is the site thus produced that much of the town, as it has increased in size, has climbed up the ranges of hills which encircle it on all sides, giving it a romantic appearance.

Its regularly laid out streets are either paved or macadamized, and are lighted with gas, supplied with water, and kept very neat and clean. Near the centre of the city is a public green, called the "Circle," from its circular form. Around it is a handsome paved promenade, shaded with trees. Around this Circle, on market days, are ranged rows of temporary stalls, and wagons from the country loaded with produce. In its vicinity are many of the oldest and finest residences, which are built of brick, and present an air of comfort and competence.

PUBLIC BUILDINGS, ETC.

The *Court-House* occupies a commanding position on the hill in the western part of the borough. There are also a number of fine churches and an academy.

On the east rises Mount Lafayette, with *Lafayette College* near its summit. This institution was founded in 1833, and has many attractive features. It is located on a beautiful eminence, overlooking the surrounding country, and its grounds cover forty acres. It has nine resident and three lecturing professors, and 100 students. Recent endowments, amounting to $300,000, have given it a new impetus. This amount has been raised mainly through the efforts of the able president, Rev. Dr. Cattell, and the liberality of A. Pardee, Esq., of Hazleton, who has contributed about $200,000. A fine new building of limestone has recently been erected, containing a cabinet with more than 8000 specimens of minerals from Pennsylvania and New Jersey alone, besides lecture-rooms and apartments for laboratories and the use of students. North of this is a new observatory, which contains a telescope of superior quality and power. Other buildings are soon to be erected and the old ones remodeled, making this college one of the best institutions of the kind in the country. Its location is peculiarly adapted for the study of those branches to which the attention of students will be more prominently directed, being in the midst of a rich mineral region, presenting a large variety of interesting fields for exploration. Here are found rare specimens of serpentine, zircons, and epidote, while north of Easton is a rock from which is obtained a rich variety of augites. A new locality, just opened, contains the sulphate of barytes, while on the south, across the Lehigh River, the Lehigh Hills are filled for miles with mines of iron. At the Phillipsburg Cut, on the south, the limestone and granite come together, a singular and unusual occurrence. This is the only granite found in this entire region.

Durham Cave, near here, contains the petrified bones of the buffalo, moose, and deer, with evidence that these animals must have inhabited this region within about a century. Here, too, at the forks of the Delaware, was the great camping-ground of the Indians in the times of Brainerd.

Mount Jefferson, the abrupt peak in the centre of the town, was an Indian lookout, where are still found arrow-heads and other Indian relics. The view of these localities from Lafayette College is grand.

Manufactures.

Among the principal manufactories of Easton is the rolling-mill and wire manufactory of Stewart & Co., at South-Easton, on the southern bank of the Lehigh, from which from 1200 to 1500 tons of iron and copper wire are made annually, and is pronounced the finest manufactured in this country. Strangers are always welcomed to see these works, which are exceedingly curious and interesting. The Glendon Iron Works are a mile and a half above Easton Centre, on the Lehigh River. Besides these are the Oxford Furnace, Cooper's Furnace, the Lehigh Cotton Factory, and the Franklin Iron Works, manufacturing nearly all kinds of agricultural implements. These various establishments give to Easton, though a somewhat antiquated German town, a busy and thriving appearance.

Bushkill Creek affords a good waterpower, upon which are more than a dozen mills and distilleries, which consume 250,000 bushels of grain, and manufacture 900,000 gallons of whisky annually.

A fine covered bridge, 600 feet long, erected in 1805 for carriage and foot travel, crosses the Delaware to Phillipsburg at the foot of Northampton street, which has alone withstood the powerful freshets that, from time to time, have carried away so many similar structures. An iron bridge across the Lehigh connects Easton with South-Easton, where is the depot of the Lehigh Valley Railroad. Over this, and crossing diagonally, the Lehigh Coal Navigation Company are erecting a new and very long bridge, to connect their road, which is nearly completed to this place, with the Morris and Essex and the New-Jersey Central, running to New-York.

Railroad Communications.

The facilities of Easton for communication with all sections of the country are numerous and excellent. It is the western terminus of the Central Railroad of New-Jersey, the Morris and Essex Railroad, and the Morris Canal. The Lehigh Valley Railroad and the Lehigh Coal Navigation Company's Railroad and Canal extend from here to the coal regions. By the Belvidere Delaware Railroad it is connected with Philadelphia below, and with Belvidere, the Water-Gap, and the Lackawanna coal regions above. The Allenton route, from Allentown through Harrisburg to Pittsburg, connects it with all points west.

No traveler should leave Easton without, once at least, climbing some of its lofty hills, and enjoying for a while the almost matchless beauty of the scene that is here spread before the vision.

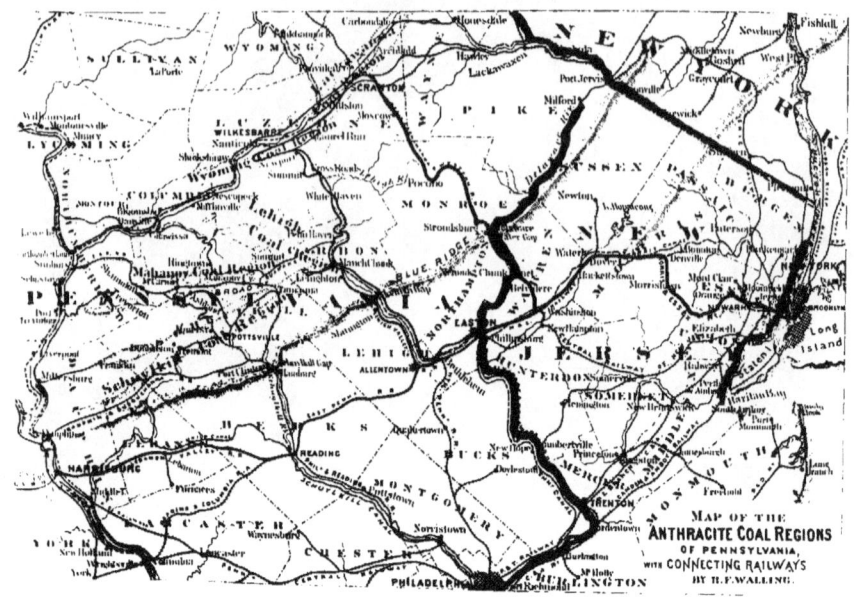

THE COAL REGIONS OF PENN-SYLVANIA.

THAT portion of Pennsylvania in which anthracite coal is found is divided into several regions, occupying three distinct basins, or long, narrow valleys, between parallel ridges of the great Appalachian system.

The first, or most southerly, is the SCHUYLKILL REGION, extending through the middle of Schuylkill county.

The second is the MIDDLE or MAHANOY REGION, north of the Schuylkill, and separated from it by Broad Mountain.

The third, being the most northerly of all, comprises the WYOMING and LACKAWANNA REGIONS, occupying a long, crescent-shaped valley, stretching north-easterly across the county of Luzerne.

The accompanying map will give a general idea of the relative positions of these regions.

The LEHIGH REGION includes the eastern extremity of the great Schuylkill basin, bordering on the Lehigh River. It also includes a number of detached basins or outlying patches of coal. It is here that the hardest and most compact variety of the anthracite, so well known as "Lehigh coal," is obtained.

The Lehigh and Schuylkill Regions have been longest and, till recently, most extensively worked, convenient access from them to market having been first established by the construction of canals and railroads down the valleys of the Lehigh and Schuylkill Rivers; but nearly the whole extent of the different basins is now accessible by railroad, and mines are being opened in all of them.

Amid such a great variety of intersecting railroads and places and objects of interest, the tourist has a choice of many different routes.

The one selected for description is, perhaps, the most picturesque that could be chosen, and in the wildness, beauty, and pleasing variety of its scenery, the ease and comfort to be found in its well-kept hotels, and the amount of useful and interesting information attainable, will, to those who have not time for a more extended journey and a more thorough examination of all the localities, prove highly satisfactory. All the interesting features of the coal formations and mining operations are to be seen on this route, together with some of the grandest and most striking scenery in America.

The route selected is *via* the Delaware, Lackawanna, and Western Railroad, through the famous Delaware Water Gap, up the Alleghany slope, over the ridge, down into the Lackawanna Valley at Scranton, thence down this valley and that of the Susquehanna to Wilkesbarre, passing through a portion of the celebrated and beautiful Wyoming Valley. From Wilkesbarre the railroad climbs by a circuitous route over the encircling mountain on the south, and then descends the Lehigh Valley, passing through a constant succession of wild and romantic scenery, and, in the vicinity of Mauch Chunk, affording an opportunity to examine some of the boldest and most successful mechanical and engineering achievements of the age.

Continuing down the beautiful valley of the Lehigh, we pass through the pleasant city of Allentown to Easton, having completed a circuit of a little over two hundred miles.

The railroads over which the described route passes, with distances, etc., are as follows :

The *Belvidere Delaware Railroad* from *Philipsburg*, opposite Easton, to *Manunka Chunk*, 17 miles.

The *Delaware, Lackawanna, and Western Railroad*, from Manunka Chunk to Scranton, 67 miles. (From New York to Scranton direct, the distance is 147 miles; namely, New York to Washington, 70 miles, Washington to Scranton, 77 miles.)

The *Lehigh and Susquehanna Railroad*, from Scranton to Wilkesbarre, 18 miles.

The *Lehigh Valley Railroad* from Wilkesbarre to Easton, 101 miles.

BELVIDERE DELAWARE RAILROAD.

EASTON TO MANUNKA CHUNK JUNCTION, 17 MILES,

From Easton, the tourist desiring to visit the Delaware Water Gap and the coal regions will cross the river to the station of the Belvidere Delaware Railroad at Phillipsburg, passing on this road as far as Manunka Chunk Junction, where the train will connect with the Delaware, Lackawanna, and Western Railroad for Scranton.

The passenger from New York to the coal regions, however, who does not wish to visit Easton, may take a more direct route from New York to Scranton by leaving the Morris and Essex Road at Washington, where it is intersected by the Delaware, Lackawanna, and Western Railroad, instead of going through to Easton. A ride of 10 miles, through the villages of Oxford Furnace and Bridgeville, would then bring us to Manunka Chunk Station.

At *Oxford Furnace*, in Oxford township, Warren Co., 9 miles from New-Hampton Junction, is an extensive iron furnace, which gives its name to the village, besides a large machine-shop, car-wheel foundry, etc. Iron ore of a rich quality is abundant in the vicinity, and is easily smelted. *Bridgeville*, 14 miles from New-Hampton, is a small village, also in Oxford township, containing a hotel, store, etc.

Leaving Phillipsburg, we wind along the east bank of the Delaware River, between mountains of limestone formation, through a charming region, with wooded hill-slopes and smooth, cultivated fields. Our first stopping-place is at

MARTIN'S CREEK.
Harmony, Warren Co., N. J.
6 m. fr. Easton.

This small stream, which gives its name to the station, empties into the Delaware on the Pennsylvania side, where there is a small village, having several stores, a tannery, and distillery, while at the station there are a few dwellings in an agricultural district. The current of the Delaware is here smooth and gentle, and contrasts strongly with its appearance as we ascend toward its source, where it becomes more rapid, and its bed rocky and uneven.

HUTCHINSONS.
Harmony, Warren Co., N. J..
8 m. fr. Easton,

On Lommasson's Creek, has two saw-mills and a few houses, in a romantic ravine east of the railway.

ROXBURY.
Harmony, Warren Co., N. J.
9 m. fr. Easton.

The village is a mile east of the station, and contains an iron foundry, a grist-mill, and several stores.

BELVIDERE.

Oxford, Warren Co., N. J.
14 *m. fr. Easton.*

Belvidere, an incorporated borough, is pleasantly located on Pequest Creek, and contains many beautiful residences, a number of churches, stores, and a fine public school. The school-building occupies a prominent site in the centre of the town, and will be recognized by its square tower and town clock. Here also is a court-house, a bank, and a number of manufactories. Among these are a large cotton mill, an iron foundry, and several saw and flour mills. The Pequest Creek here has a fall of about 50 feet, affording abundant water-power. Beyond the station the road is cut in the side of the Manunka Chunk Mountain. Taylor's Island, beneath in the Delaware, is a wooded and delightfully pleasant spot.

MANUNKA CHUNK.

Oxford, Warren Co., N.J.
75 *m. fr. N. Y. Fr. Scranton,* **67**.

This is the junction of the Delaware and Belvidere with the Delaware, Lackawanna, and Western Railroad. Passengers from Easton for the Water Gap here change cars, passing up an inclined covered way to the station of the Delaware, Lackawanna, and Western Railroad. A few rods south, that road is seen emerging from the Voss Gap Tunnel, cut through the Manunka Chunk Mountain, a distance of nearly 1000 feet. A small stream runs through the tunnel beside the track. Ten miles south-east from here is the junction with the Morris and Essex Railroad at Washington. New-Hampton, the junction with the Central Railway of New-Jersey, and the commencement of the Delaware, Lackawanna, and Western Railroad, is **14 miles** south-east.

Delaware, Lackawanna, and Western Railroad.

MANUNKA CHUNK TO SCRANTON, 67 MILES.

The route here passes along the east bank of the Delaware, through fine, fertile meadows and smoothly rounded hills, cultivated to their summits.

DELAWARE STATION.

Knowlton, Warren Co., N. J.
82 *m. fr. N. Y. Fr. Scranton,* **65.**

Here trains from both directions stop 15 minutes for dinner. Soon after leaving here the railroad crosses the Delaware into the State of Pennsylvania, over a fine bridge, several hundred feet long.

COLUMBIA.

Upper Mt. Bethel, Northampton Co., Pa.
85 *m. fr. N. Y. Fr. Scranton,* **62.**

The village of Columbia is on the east side of the river, at the mouth of Paulins Kill. Here are extensive tanneries, limestone quarries, and lime-kilns. The village around the station is called Dill's Ferry.

SLATEFORD.

Mt. Bethel, Northampton Co., Pa.
88 *m. fr N. Y. Fr. Scranton,* **59.**

A small village where are extensive slate quarries. We now are under the shadow of the towering Blue Mountains, and soon enter the "Water Gap." The traveler will now find his attention fully engrossed by the wild magnificence and grandeur of the scenery.

DELAWARE WATER GAP STATION.

Smithfield, Monroe Co., Pa.
90 *m. fr. N. Y. Fr. Scranton,* **57.**

Here we will diverge from the monotony of simply describing the stations as we pass, and speak of the Delaware River itself, and its romantic passage to the sea, as well as of the places of interest in the immediate vicinity of the "Gap."

The Delaware River,

Called by the Indians "*Makeriskitton,*" rises in New-York, on the western declivity of the Catskill Mountains, by two branches, which, after flowing south-westerly for more than 70 miles through deep and narrow mountain ravines, unite at the village of Hancock, on the Erie Railway, near the north-east corner of Pennsylvania.

From thence, for 75 miles, it flows south-easterly, forming the boundary between the States of New-York and Pennsylvania to Port Jervis, at the north-west corner of New-Jersey, and between New-Jersey and Pennsylvania below that point to its mouth. Just below Port Jervis it reaches the foot of the *Blue Ridge* or *Kittatinny* Mountain, also called in New-York the *Shawangunk* Mountain.

Here its course again changes to the south-west, and it runs along the foot of the mountain as if seeking a passage, which at length it finds at the Water Gap. Turning toward the south, it passes through the Gap, again turns south-west, and at Easton, 27 miles below, it sweeps around to the south-east, passing through the ranges known as South Mountain in Pennsylvania, and Scott Mountain, Pohatcong Mountain, etc., in New-Jersey. Continuing in a south-easterly direction, it descends rapidly over a rocky bed in the vicinity of Trenton: then, 5 miles below, at Bordentown, bends again to the south-west, where, having gradually increased in volume and size, it has become a fine, navigable river, half a mile in width. Twenty-five miles below Bordentown it skirts the wharves of the city of Philadelphia, bearing upon its surface ships and steamers of the largest size, and finally empties its waters into the Delaware Bay, 40 miles below Philadelphia.

Its entire length, from its source in the mountains to the Bay, is about 300 miles. The scenery above the Water Gap presents a remarkable contrast to that below it, being wild, rugged, and romantic, while the river below the Gap flows through a rich, level, and fertile region, and its banks are lined with thriving and populous villages, towns, and cities.

Scenery at the Gap.

Of the Delaware Water Gap and the scenery in its immediate vicinity but a feeble and imperfect impression can be obtained through the medium of language. It must be visited and thoroughly explored by those who would obtain an adequate idea of its magnificent beauty and grandeur.

The topography of the mountains and hills of Pennsylvania presents some most curious and remarkable features which have never been fully explained. Running generally in long, parallel ridges, they are frequently broken up into a few short zigzags, and then stretch off again for many miles in continuous, nearly uniformly sloping, ridges, having the general character of immense embankments.

The gaps through which rivers find their way are generally where these breaks in direction occur, and it would almost seem that they had been weakened or actually broken at these places by some lateral force, and thus have allowed the running water to cut its way through with more or less ease.

Professor Rogers, who conducted the great geological survey of the State, traces a nearly uniform law in these cases, namely, that the ridges on the east of the fissures are displaced to the north of the range of those on the west. We shall see, in passing through the Delaware Gap, that the New-Jersey portion of the mountain is several hundred feet north-west of the range of the Pennsylvania portion.

The distance through the mountain is about 2 miles, and the banks rise precipitously to the height of 1600 feet, leaving at the south-east entrance scarcely room for a road beneath the overhanging rocks. The rock strata lie at a considerable angle with the plane of the horizon, as may be distinctly seen from the car-windows. They are made up principally of sandstone and conglomerate rock. The causes which have produced this mighty upheaval of these immense masses of solid rock, and have so inclined them out of their original level direction, are a subject of curious speculation; but, as geologists have not yet obtained sufficient evidence to become fully decided on these points, we must for the present leave the matter in their hands.

The places of interest among these mountains are numerous, many of them connected with the earlier history of this region, especially rich in *Indian* legends, and eventful of Indian history.

Ascending the Kittatinny Mountain, on the left, by a steep and rugged path, the *Moss Cataract* is a favorite lounging-place. Here a small stream of clear, ice-cold water tumbles down a succession of moss-covered rocks, scattering its cooling spray in the most refreshing manner, while the music of its fall may be heard for a long distance.

"*Lover's Leap*" affords a beautiful and commanding view of the Gap and its surroundings, and that from *Prospect Rock* is beyond description. This rock is a rugged table of brown stone, which is only reached after a rough and tiresome walk up a winding path nearly two miles long; but, when reached, the view amply repays the toil which must be undergone to enjoy it.

Toward the right stands the grim old Jersey Mountain in all its solemn grandeur, losing itself in the distance in the continuous range of the Blue Ridge, of which it is simply the cut end of one of its severed portions. Down in the valley the river winds its way over beds of rock, its blue outline broken here and there by the foam of the rapids.

Toward the left and below us we see the railroad station, with the road winding around the foot of the Pennsylvania Mountain, and above it the Kittatinny House, where visitors can signal friends who have climbed to this lofty height. This hotel is a very popular resort, and has among its guests many who stand high in social, financial, and political circles. It is located on a high ledge in the Gap itself, and is reached from the station by carriages which are always in waiting for the accommodation of travelers.

Leaving the Gap, we cross Broadhead's Creek, a wild and romantic stream, and pass on through a deep cut in the solid rock called "Rock Difficult" from the labor required in excavating it. This rock resembles flint, and $80,000 were expended in cutting a passage through it.

STROUDSBURG.

Stroudsburg, Monroe Co., F 1.
94 *m. fr. N. Y. Fr. Scranton*, **53.**

The shire-town of Monroe county, on the north bank of the Smithfield Creek. The village is seen a mile south of the station, in a pleasant valley. It is laid out on a single street, and has a court-house, a jail, and other county buildings, with a population of about 1500. Here are several flour-mills. We have now left the rugged mountains several miles behind, and roll along a more level region, soon again coming alongside of Broadhead's Creek, a winding stream abounding with trout.

SPRAGUEVILLE.
Stroudsburg, Monroe Co., Pa.,
99 *m. fr. N. Y. Fr. Scranton,* **48,**
Is situated on Broadhead Creek, in a wooded region surrounded by hills. Here is a tannery, a flour-mill, a church, and a small village. Commencing at Spragueville, the grade ascends, at the rate of 65 feet to the mile, to the summit of the Pocono Mountain, a distance of 25 miles. This is the eastern slope of the great Alleghany range. Much of the region we now traverse is a wilderness covered with forests, having here and there a clearing with a small village on the line of the railroad, or a few scattered huts of woodmen.

HENRYVILLE,
Paradise, Monroe Co., Pa.,
102 *m. fr. N. Y. Fr. Scranton,* **45,**
Is down in the valley to the left, and contains a saw-mill, a church, several stores, and dwellings. We are now passing gradually up the Alleghany slope, and, as we rise, we overlook an extensive wooded country, with here and there a farm-house or a cabin. Pines and oaks cover this slope, the spurs of which are here called the Pocono Mountains. Large quantities of wood and timber are sent from this station.

OAKLAND.
Paradise, Monroe Co., Pa.
107 *m. fr. N. Y. Fr. Scranton,* **40.**
A small station. A hotel is being built here. The village is a mile east, and contains a large tannery. Soon after leaving here the railway sweeps around to the south along the side of the mountain, affording a fine view on the left of the Blue Mountains, with the Water Gap in the distance, and the broad valley between. On the right, the view is shut in by the Pocono Mountains.

PARADISE.
Paradise, Monroe Co., Pa.,
110 *m. fr. N. Y. Fr. Scranton,* **37,**
Is a small station where trains stop for water. Here are two or three dwellings of woodmen in the wilderness. We now pass on up the steep ascent, and through the Pocono Tunnel, near the summit of Pocono Mountain. The view from this high elevation is magnificent, stretching over a vast wilderness, 30 miles in extent. Toward the south, the Blue Ridge bounds the horizon for a long distance, presenting the appearance of an immense extended embankment, in which the well-defined sides of the Delaware Water Gap distinctly appear. Nearer to us are seen a succession of smaller ridges of the same mountain system. Here we make another sweep around to the west, and arrive at

POCONO FORK.
Coolbaugh, Monroe Co., Pa.
113 *m. fr. N. Y. Fr. Scranton,* **34.**
So called from its being the diverging place of two carriage-roads, the one leading north to Sterling, and the other north-west to Clifton. Here are a few dwellings in a lonely region. Pine, oak, ash, and cherry are the principal kinds of timber that abound, many of the trees measuring 7 and 8 feet in diameter, and rising to the height of more than 100 feet. Hem-

lock of great size is also found in this vicinity.

After passing this station we begin to cross small streams running toward the west, which are tributary to the Lehigh River. The course of the railroad changes to a little west of north.

TOBYHANNA.

Coolbaugh, Monroe Co., Pa.,
120 *m. fr. N. Y. Fr. Scranton,* **27,**

Is on the top of the mountain, a small village which has been built up by the lumber business. On the right is a small lake, usually covered with logs, and on its west bank is a large steam saw-mill with immense piles of lumber, near the railroad. Coolbaugh has a church, a store, and thirty or forty dwellings. The soil here is barren, and but little of it has been cleared. The grade now changes to a descending one, and we pass on through rugged forest scenery for many miles.

GOULDSBOROUGH.

Sterling, Wayne Co., Pa.,
126 *m. fr. N. Y. Fr. Scranton,* **21,**

In the south-west corner of Wayne county, is in a lumber region, and has a steam saw-mill, a hotel, and a few dwellings. Large quantities of bark are sent from this station for tanning hides. The streams in this vicinity abound with trout. The village of Clifton is three or four miles west of this station. A few miles further on we enter the valley of Roaring Brook, and continue in it on a descending grade till we reach Scranton. It is very small when we first encounter it, but rapidly increases as we descend.

MOSCOW.

Madison, Luzerne Co., Pa.
134 *m. fr. N.Y. Fr. Scranton,* **13**
HOTELS—*Moscow, and Delaware Lackawanna, and Western.*

A village of greater pretensions than any we have passed since leaving Stroudsburg. It has, however, grown up within nine years. It is engaged principally in the lumber business. Here are two churches and several stores. Numbers of sportsmen visit this locality to enjoy the hunting and fishing. Large quantities of lumber are sent south from here. As we descend toward the Lackawanna we find the country more and more cleared up and settled, although the numerous stumps that dot the fields show that not many years ago this was a primeval forest.

DUNNING.

Madison, Luzerne Co., Pa.
137 *m. fr. N. Y. Fr. Scranton,* **10.**

Here is a very large tannery and a saw-mill, around which has grown up a small village. On the other side, or east of Roaring Brook, the Pennsylvania Coal Company's Railroad will be noticed, extending from the Susquehanna River, near Pittston, to Hawley on the Delaware and Hudson Canal, forty-seven miles. This road was completed in 1850, and consists of two tracks, diverging in some parts to a distance of two or three miles; one, called the *loaded track,* being for the conveyance of cars loaded with coal; and the other, called the *light track,* for the return of the empty cars. The company owning this road mine, ship to market, and sell immense quantities of anthracite coal. The *Hawley*

Branch of the Erie Railway, constructed in 1862, extends from Hawley to Lackawaxen on the Erie Railway 22 miles, affording an outlet to the seaboard all the way by railroad, besides that of the Canal. The road has been provided with engines and cars sufficient to meet the requirements of a coal traffic which amounted, in 1866, to about 700,000 tons. This was forwarded over the Erie Railway to Newburg, Piermont, and Jersey City.

GREENVILLE.
Jefferson, Luzerne Co., Pa.
139 *m. fr. N. Y. Fr. Scranton,* **8.**

A small way-station, with several saw-mills. Passing through a short tunnel, we now enter upon a rapidly descending grade, requiring no steam to propel the train, but rather an application of the brakes to moderate its speed.

On the right we pass a large colliery, at what is called "The Notch," and on the opposite side an iron mine, having a branch track running to it, on the steep bank of a ravine, in which runs the Roaring Brook, and which, just before reaching Scranton, tumbles down a rocky precipice, forming a beautiful and romantic cascade.

Soon *Scranton*, far beneath us in the valley of the Lackawanna River, comes in view with its iron furnaces and smoking chimneys, which we pass on approaching the depot. The contrast now presented between the vast uninhabited region which we have traversed and this pleasant valley is very striking. Here the traveler may well linger and spend several days in visiting the immense iron works, coal mines, and various objects of interest that abound in this locality.

SCRANTON.
Scranton, Luzerne Co., Pa.
147 *miles from New-York.*
HOTEL—*Wyoming House.*

The Lackawanna Valley owes its earliest explorations to the Moravians, who fled from Moravia, in Germany, to escape persecution, and made the first settlement in Pennsylvania in 1740. That part of it upon which *Scranton* is located was first known as "Capouse Meadow," from the name of the chief of a tribe of the Delawares who dwelt upon these flats.

It lies in the valley of the Lackawanna River, with the Moosic Mountains on the east, and the Lackawannock on the west, rising around it by gentle slopes at first, and by more steep and precipitous elevations in the further ascent. Roaring Brook, or the Nayang River, rising among the mountains on the south-east, winds its way downward to this valley, and here unites with the Lackawanna. Upon the banks of this stream, Philip Abbott, in 1788, built the first grist-mill in the neighborhood, which supplied the demands of Luzerne and several adjacent counties.

The earliest settlers in this valley were emigrants from Windham county, Connecticut. In 1798, Benjam'n and Ebenezer Slocum, brothers of little *Frances*, whose abduction from Wyoming when she was but five years of age is a matter of tradition, settled here, and bought 1700 acres of land, including the old grist-mill; erected a saw-mill, a forge, and a distillery. This tract was long known as the Slocum Farm.

The preëminence of the Slocum Brothers here caused the name of "Slocum Hollow" to take the place of "Capouse Meadow." In 1810, there were but three dwellings in the town, though a post-office had been established, the mail being brought on horseback over the mountains from Easton once a week.

The city of *Scranton* owes its growth mainly to the efforts of the friends of the "Drinker Railroad" to get it constructed. *William Henry*, who was the first man that fully appreciated the importance of a speedy communication with market by railroad, in partnership with *Edward Armstrong*, purchased here 800 acres of land. Soon after, Armstrong died, and in August, 1840, *George* and *Selden Scranton* and *Sanford Grant* came here, and entered into partnership with Mr. Henry, purchasing the entire Slocum estate.

In September, this company commenced the erection of a blast furnace. The products of the furnace were sent to market by the Delaware and Hudson Canal or by the North Branch and Tide-Water Canal, but in both cases had to be conveyed miles by wagon to reach these avenues of transportation.

In 1844, the first rolling-mill was completed, and here, in 1845, the T rail for railroads was first made in the United States. Two years after this, the Erie Railroad Company contracted with the Scrantons for 1200 tons of iron rails, and thenceforward the demands upon this new company constantly increased.

The honor of the inception of a railroad from Great Bend to the Delaware Water Gap belongs to Colonel George W. Scranton. In 1853, the present line was adopted, and in 1856 the first locomotive rolled from Scranton to the Delaware River. Since then the growth of the place has been most rapid, and the larger part of this city has been built.

A fine view of the city is obtained from the high bluff near the Baptist church in Hyde Park, where the charming and interesting panorama that is spread out before him will amply compensate the tourist for the trouble of the ascent.

The huge, round, slate-roofed engine-house resembles somewhat the Roman Colosseum, while the immense furnaces and work-shops, the numerous fine private residences, elegant churches, and handsome stores make up a busy and brilliant foreground, which contrasts finely with the deep green of the surrounding forests, and the purple of the sharply defined mountain ranges which shut in this wonderful valley.

Collieries may be seen in different directions on the sides of the valleys, with mountains of coal-dirt heaped up around them, and long trains of cars loaded with the "black diamonds" winding along the numerous railroads.

Scranton was incorporated as a city in 1866, and includes within its limits the villages of Hyde Park and Providence, comprising twelve wards in all. Its streets are wide and regularly laid out. It is lighted with gas and supplied with water, has four smelting furnaces, two rolling-mills, two ax and scythe manufactories, two stove foundries, three planing-mills, four banks, four flour-mills, three saw-mills, and six breweries and distilleries. There are also twenty-four churches and four academies.

A horse-railroad connects the centre of the city of Scranton with Providence, its most northerly portion. In

Scranton is also the junction of the Delaware, Lackawanna, and Western Railroad with the Lackawanna and Bloomsburg and the Lehigh Coal and Navigation Company's Railroad, affording railway communications with all parts of the country.

IRON WORKS.

No one who visits Scranton should fail to visit the iron works here. They are immense in size, and capable of smelting 70,000 tons of metal annually. Their size may be inferred from that of the "*boshes*," which are fifteen, seventeen, eighteen, and even twenty feet in diameter and fifty feet high.

Into these furnaces air is forced by double engines with connected leverbeams. Two of these are of eight hundred and two of twelve hundred horsepower. But one larger pair is to be found in the country.

Steam cylinders of the first pair are fifty-four inches in diameter with ten feet stroke. The large fly-wheel which regulates the movements of this enormous apparatus weighs 40,000 pounds. The other pair of engines has a flywheel twenty-eight feet in diameter, weighing 75,000 pounds.

Just above these furnaces are the puddling and rolling-mills. The ore, most of which is brought from Cornwall, Pennsylvania, is first smelted and run into pig-iron, after which it is ready for "puddling."

This process consists in heating the bars of pig-iron to a high degree, and then working the metal by a sort of kneading process with iron bars until it crumbles and dissolves, becoming a seetning melted mass. After continuing the heating and puddling for a while longer, it becomes less fluid and appears "sticky," when it is massed into balls weighing about a hundred pounds, which are then taken by boys and conveyed upon little wagons called "buggies," to the "crocodile," which, with its massive iron jaws constantly opening and closing, squeezes them into cylindrical shapes convenient for the *rolling*, which immediately follows.

By this process, which consists in passing the masses of hot iron between a succession of rollers, they are converted into long, slender bars; these are cut into pieces about three feet in length. These pieces are then placed in piles about eight inches square, with those bars which are made of the best iron upon the top, to make the top of the rail, and inferior iron in the centre. They are then placed in furnaces and subjected to an intense heat, until the separate bars forming a pile are all fused together, so that they can be handled as one mass. Each pile is then rolled between rollers of the required form into a rail, which, being sawed off the proper length while still hot, straightened and notched for the spikes, is ready for use.

These mills and furnaces consume a hundred thousand tons of coal annually, and employ about 1200 men. Their appearance by night, when each chimney is surmounted by a crown of flame, and the gleaming fires and luminous iron contrasting strongly with the surrounding darkness, reminds one of Vulcan's infernal realm and the mythic forges over which he presided.

The visitor, as he gazes on the massive furnace stacks, pouring out day after day huge piles of crude or finished iron, from the ponderous bar to the slender bolt, and sees the smooth yet resistless motion of one of the largest stationary engines on the American continent, can not fail to be interested and gratified especially with the indications of skill, enterprise, and good management everywhere displayed.

The most important and interesting feature of Scranton is the fact that it lies in the centre of a *great coal region*, from which will be drawn the source of motive-power not only for the works here, but for all parts of the country. Numerous collieries are already opened throughout the region. The traveler should not omit to visit some of the mines in the vicinity. The superintendents of these are generally intelligent and kind, and will use every endeavor to make a visit into the mines pleasant and free from danger or annoyance.

A description of the different modes of mining the coal, which, though simple, are very interesting, will be found in another part of this Guide.

Lehigh and Susquehanna Railroad.

SCRANTON TO WILKESBARRE, 18 MILES.

THE railroad between these two points is owned in part by the *Union Coal Company*, and in part by the *Nanticoke Railroad Company*. The Lehigh Coal and Navigation Company, who own the Lehigh and Susquehanna Railroad, have, however, purchased nearly the entire stock of the latter company, and have obtained the exclusive right to run freight and passenger trains, and all coal trains running west over the former company's road, which extends from a point on the Nanticoke Railroad about five miles east of Wilkesbarre, to connect with the Delaware and Hudson Canal Company's Railroad at Providence, six miles beyond Scranton.

The Lehigh Coal and Navigation Company have recently completed their line from Wilkesbarre to Mauch Chunk, and have nearly completed its extension from Mauch Chunk to Easton, thus forming a continuous line from Scranton to Easton. The latter part of this line is to be laid with Bessemer steel rails.

SCRANTON STATION.

The new passenger station of the Lehigh and Susquehanna Railroad is west of that of the Delaware, Lackawanna, and Western Railroad, and on the bank of the Lackawanna River. Leaving this station, we pass along the east bank of this stream, in full view of the Scranton iron works and the city itself, rising along the slopes of the valley. Near the river and railway we pass a number of coal-mines with their coal-breakers and immense piles of coal-dirt and slate. It is the coal that constitutes the chief wealth of this valley, the agricultural resources of it being only partially developed. On the left we pass the Wyoming and Lackawanna Coal Company's Mines; and across the river, on the right, are seen the mines of the Delaware, Lackawanna, and Western Railroad Company.

MINOOKA.

Lackawanna, Luzerne Co., Pa.
3m.fr.Scranton. Fr.Wilkesbarre, **15.**

A small mining village in the vicinity of several collieries, containing a few stores and a hotel.

SPRING BROOK.

Pittston, Luzerne Co., Pa.,
6*m.fr.Scranton. Fr.Wilkesbarre,***12,**
On Spring Brook, a small tributary of the Lackawanna, is a wild settlement of miners, some eight miles south-east of the station, beyond the mountains, which form the boundary of the coal basis.

PITTSTON.

Pittston, Luzerne Co., Pa.,
10*m.fr.Scranton. Fr.Wilkesbarre,***8,**
Is seen in the valley, on the right of the railroad, as we approach the station. It is a thriving town, situated just below where the Lackawanna River empties into the Susquehanna, and at the head of the Wyoming Valley, in the vicinity of rich mines of coal, and owes its rapid growth chiefly to the mining operations of the Pennsylvania Coal Company. Here are extensive iron works, a national bank, several churches, and fine residences. The West Branch Canal passes through Pittston. On the west of the town rises the beautiful Lackawannock range of mountains.

THE WYOMING VALLEY,

Which we have now entered, is replete with historic associations, carrying us back to the hardships of its early settlers, and the terrible and bloody struggle for American independence. It lies along the banks of the Susquehanna, between two parallel ranges of mountains, extending from the northeast to the south-west, and rising on the east to the height of 1000 feet, and on the west. about 800 feet. While within these ranges all the land is underlaid with a greater or less number of veins of coal, outside of them none is found. The Wyoming valley is about 3 miles wide and 25 long, and abounds in romantic scenery and pleasant drives.

Like the Lackawanna, this valley was settled by emigrants from Connecticut, who were opposed in their possession of the soil by some of the Pennsylvania landholders, and this resulted in what was called the "Yankee and Pennamite war." What the Pennsylvanians desired was to establish here a kind of feudal system, retaining the social and political power in the hands of a few. The "Yankees" could never submit to such principles, and hence the animosity between the two parties was exceedingly bitter, resulting in embarrassment. to the settlers, and in bloodshed.

The war of the Revolution, however, put an end to these animosities, when common liberties were at stake, and common dangers imperiled the lives and interests of all. The British, in 1778, had determined to make use of the Indians in this contest; and, at the solicitation of their agents, a body of Iroquois joined a band of tories under Colonel John Butler, and advanced toward Wyoming, easily capturing Fort Wintermoot, at the head of the valley, which contained a population of several thousand, but had contributed so largely to the patriot army that few able-bodied men were left for its defense. The account of the conflict is as follows: As the ruthless invaders approached, the women and children flocked from the surrounding region to a fort near the present site of Wilkesbarre, called "Forty Fort," while 300 men, with a few boys, under Zebulon Butler, advanced to meet the enemy.

The Americans fought bravely, and even gained ground, till one of the officers, wishing to take a more favorable position in the rear, bade his men "fall back." The order was misunderstood, and the unfortunate word "retreat" passed along the lines. Panic seized the soldiers, and a general flight ensued. Many were shot and tomahawked as they ran, some threw themselves into the river, a few escaped to the fort, where the helpless women were screaming with terror. That night the Indians held possession of the battlefield, and tortured their prisoners with all the cruelties that savage cunning could invent. Captain Bidlack was thrown alive on burning coals, and kept there with pitchforks till he expired. Six prisoners were ranged near a stone on the river bank, and held by savages while Queen Esther, an old Seneca half-breed, walked round them in a circle, singing the death-song like an infuriated demon, striking them with her club and hatchet till every man was killed. This stone is a conglomerate boulder, about a foot and a half high, and still is called Queen Esther's Rock.

The next day the fort was invested, and surrendered to the British leader on his promise to protect its defenseless occupants; but no sooner were the savages admitted, than they glutted their thirst for blood by tomahawking and scalping all whom they met. The unfortunate people of Wyoming were compelled to flee to distant and securer settlements. Few survived the horrors of the flight. Some escaped the red man's knife only to find a slower death from exposure and fatigue. Distracted mothers hurried their children through the wilderness; and, when their little ones fainted and died, bore their lifeless bodies many a weary mile to save them from the hungry wolves. Such were the frightful scenes that laid this lovely valley desolate, and have hallowed its name and soil.

A prominent object of interest in the vicinity of Pittston is Campbell's Ledge, a crowning bluff of the mountain which rises between the Lackawanna and Susquehanna Rivers. Its name is said to be derived from a tradition that a Mr. Campbell once leaped from it to escape pursuing Indians. Others think that it is named from the poet Campbell, who made this valley illustrious through his *Gertrude of Wyoming*. The view from this ledge is one of the most complete to be found in the whole vicinity.

YATESVILLE.
Jenkins, Luzerne Co., Pa.
11 m. fr. Scranton. Fr. Wilkesbarre, 7.

A small mining village in the vicinity of the Union and Pine Ridge Collieries, which are seen on the left of the railway.

MILL CREEK.
Plains, Luzerne Co., Pa.
15 m. fr. Scranton, Fr. Wilkesbarre, 3.

On Mill Creek, a tributary of the Susquehanna. Here are a colliery and several saw-mills. In this vicinity are some good farms. The mountains on either side of the valley form a beautiful feature of the landscape. As the train approaches Wilkesbarre, we pass under a number of coal-shutes, where the coal from the neighboring mines is loaded into the boats of the Susquehanna Canal, or railroad cars, to be sent east and south.

WILKESBARRE.
Wilkesbarre, Luzerne Co., Pa.
18 m. fr. Scranton.
HOTELS.—*Wyoming* and *Phenix Houses.*

The capital of Luzerne county is situated on the left bank of the North Branch of the Susquehanna River, in the beautiful Wyoming Valley, commanding a fine view of river and mountain scenery. It is laid out with considerable regularity, having wide, well-shaded streets, with a public square and court-house near the centre. It was settled by the Susquehanna Land Company of Connecticut in 1773, and in some respects resembles many of the quiet New-England towns. It contains several churches and academies, three or four banks, a large rolling-mill, an iron furnace, a scale manufactory, and other works of less importance.

What gives greater prominence to this town, however, is its coal works, the beds here being among the thickest in the State. Above the town are 3 large collieries, while below are 4 or 5 more, from which immense quantities of coal are dug annually, and sent to market.

In the rooms of the Historical Society is a museum of curiosities and historical relics which will interest a visitor.

Among the principal attractions for tourists is "*Prospect Rock*," upon the mountain directly back of Wilkesbarre. It is accessible by means of a carriage to within 200 yards. The view includes a large part of the entire valley, and is one of such rare beauty that, once seen, can never be forgotten. So varied and extended is the prospect, so rich in all that can inspire and fill the soul with the love of the beautiful, that one seems to be translated to another sphere while looking down upon this magnificent panorama. In its vicinity is a fine hotel for the accommodation of those wishing to spend some time among the mountains.

The *Wyoming Monument*, erected to commemorate the great disaster of the battle of Wyoming, and to preserve and honor the names of the brave soldiers who fell, as well as those who survived, stands near the old battlefield, within the township of Kingston, on the right bank of the river. It was erected in 1832 through the exertions of the ladies of Wyoming, and is a granite obelisk 62½ feet high. Upon marble slabs in front and on two sides are inscriptions recording the events of the battle and the names of the fallen, under the line of Horace, "Dulce et decorum est pro patriâ mori." A little below this monument is the site of old Fort Forty.

Harvey's Lake, about 12 miles north-west of Wilkesbarre, under the slope of the Alleghany Mountains, is a favorite resort. This lake abounds with fish, while the surrounding woodlands contain deer and a variety of wild game. The view here is very beautiful. A hotel called the Lake House has been erected in its vicinity.

A bridge across the Susquehanna connects Wilkesbarre with *Kingston*. Horse-cars and omnibuses are in waiting at the station of the Lehigh and Susquehanna Railroad on arrival of trains, to convey passengers to various parts of the town.

The Lackawanna and Bloomsbury Railroad, passing through Kingston, on the opposite side of the Susquehanna River, connects it with Scranton on the east and Northumberland on the west, where connections are made with the great through lines, north, south, east, and west.

LEHIGH VALLEY RAILROAD.

WILKESBARRE TO EASTON, 101 MILES.

THIS railroad is now completed from Easton to Wilkesbarre, and an extension is to be constructed from Wilkesbarre, up the North Branch of the Susquehanna River, to Waverley, on the Erie Railway, in New-York, where it will connect with lines running north, east, and west.

From Wilkesbarre to Easton, after making a great detour to the west, in order to get over the mountain ridge, it runs parallel with the Lehigh and Susquehanna Railroad, generally on the opposite river bank. The two roads cross each other several times between their terminations.

SOUTH-WILKESBARRE.
Wilkesbarre, Luzerne Co., Pa.
175 *m. fr. N. Y. Fr. Wilkesbarre,* **1.**
In the southern part of the town, on the Susquehanna Canal, which here for a while runs parallel with the railroad.

SUGAR NOTCH.
Hanover, Luzerne Co., Pa.
172 *m. fr. N. Y. Fr. Wilkesbarre,* **4.**
Here is the Sugar Notch Colliery of "Parish & Thomas," with a small number of dwellings. We are now passing up an ascending grade, which varies from 60 to 96 feet to the mile in climbing to the summit of the mountains, and often through deep cuts in the solid rock.

WARRIOR RUN.
Hanover, Luzerne Co., Pa.
170 *m. fr. N. Y. Fr. Wilkesbarre,* **6.**
This station derives its name from a small creek running into the Susquehanna.

NEWPORT STATION.
Newport, Luzerne Co., Pa.
167 *m. fr. N. Y. Fr. Wilkesbarre,* **9.**
The view at this station is magnificent beyond description. The railroad has here climbed nearly to the summit of the mountain, and the entire Wyoming Valley, in all its romantic beauty, is spread out in a broad panorama. The silvery Susquehanna may be seen meandering among the green meadows and fertile fields for twenty miles, en-

tering the mountain ridge, which forms the north wall of this lovely valley, through the Lackawannock Gap, a little north of Pittston, and leaving it again at the Nanticoke Gap, near Shickshinny. Pleasant towns and villages are interspersed throughout the valley, with an occasional colliery to indicate the mineral wealth beneath the surface, and the whole ground-picture is inclosed in a beautiful border or frame of blue mountains. On the left Solomon's Gap is seen, where the Lehigh and Susquehanna Railway originally conveyed their cars directly over the mountains by a series of planes. This route is only used now for heavy coal-trains, the necessity of the planes for the lighter trains being avoided by a detour for the purpose of making a gradual ascent somewhat similar to the one we have just made, its direction, however, being toward the east instead of the west. The great loups formed by the two roads are thus some nine miles each in length, while they only accomplish a direct distance of two or three miles.

FAIRVIEW.
Wright, Luzerne Co., Pa.
159 *m.fr. N.Y. Fr. Wilkesbarre,* **17.**

On the summit of the mountain. Here we cross the Lehigh and Susquehanna Railroad. A wild view stretches far southward, among mountains wooded with oak and pine, uninhabited, save by a few woodmen, and forming a vast wilderness. We now begin to descend, winding romantically around wooded slopes; and in places the grade is such that the brakes are occasionally applied to the train to moderate its speed.

NESCOPEC STATION.
Wright, Luzerne Co., Pa.
156 *m.fr. N.Y. Fr. Wilkesbarre,* **20**.

So-called from its being the junction of the Nescopec Branch Railroad. It is also a stopping-place for water. A few cabins of workmen, recently erected and unpainted, constitute the present settlement. Again we cross the Lehigh and Susquehanna Railroad.

CRANBERRY MARSH.
Denison, Luzerne Co., Pa.
149 *m.fr. N.Y. Fr. Wilkesbarre,* **27.**

Here is a small station with a few rude huts. We now cross a marsh on an embankment, which, a short time after completion, sank into the marsh 65 feet, pressing up the clay on both sides of it.

The rock formation here is a red sandstone, with sandstone shales. Lumber to some extent is sent from this locality. Soon we come in sight of the Lehigh River, along whose bank we proceed the remainder of the way to Easton.

WHITE HAVEN,
Denison, Luzerne Co., Pa.,
146 *m.fr. N.Y. Fr. Wilkesbarre,* **30,**
HOTEL—The *Phœnix,*

Is a flourishing borough situated on the Lehigh River, 25 miles above Mauch Chunk. Its settlement was commenced in 1835, and it received its name from Josiah White. The lumber business is the most prominent. Keck & Childs have a large steam saw-mill and lumber-yard, and Wallace & Briesch an extensive car manufactory here. The village lies upon the hillside, overlooking the river, and contains four churches, some pleasant residences, and a population of about 1500.

After leaving this station we cross the Lehigh, obtaining a fine view up and down its current. Immense quantities of logs and rafts are seen floating upon the surface of the ponds, formed by two large dams across this stream. The Lehigh and Susquehanna Railway runs parallel with the Lehigh Valley, upon the opposite side of the river.

TANNERY.
Kidder, Carbon Co., Pa.
144 *m.fr. N.Y. Fr. Wilkesbarre,* **32.**

So-called because here is located Holcomb's large tannery. There are also extensive lumber nooks at this point, and a little further on Gruld's grist-mill.

HICKORY RUN.
Kidder, Carbon Co., Pa.
141 *m.fr. N.Y. Fr. Wilkesbarre,* **35.**

The Hickory Run is a small stream emptying into the Lehigh, upon which are a number of large saw-mills. We notice as we pass down the river the remains of numerous dams. These dams were erected by the Lehigh Coal and Navigation Company as feeders for their canal, which was formerly in operation as far as White Haven; but the great freshet of 1862 swept away very many of these, and they have never been repaired further north than Mauch Chunk. The canal, however, has been replaced by the Lehigh and Susquehanna Railroad, belonging to the same company, who have also recently extended their railroad from Mauch Chunk to Easton, making a continuous road from Scranton *via* Wilkesbarre to Philadelphia and New-York. The scenery in this vicinity is wild and romantic, the river winding its way between high mountains, over a pebbly and rocky bed, skirted on each side by a railway.

MUD RUN.
Kidder, Carbon Co., Pa.
139 *m.fr. N.Y. Fr. Wilkesbarre,* **37.**

Here a wild mountain stream enters the Lehigh. Upon it are several saw-mills. The picturesqueness of the scenery along the entire extent of the Lehigh River, particularly of the portion above Mauch Chunk, is unsurpassed.

ROCKPORT.
Lausanne, Carbon Co., Pa.
136 *m.fr. N.Y. Fr. Wilkesbarre,* **40.**

This village is upon the opposite side of the river, in a ravine, and has grown up in connection with the operations of the Buck Mountain Coal Company, whose mines are four miles distant, at a place called Clifton. Rockport is merely the point where the coal is transferred to the railroad and canal-boats for the East. Further on we pass through some deep cuts in the solid rock, so directly under the shadow of the mountains that we seem shut in from the rest of the world. And for a time we are fully content to be; so for the mountains, with their green foliage and bold grandeur, rising above the winding and beautiful river, present a series of ever-changing landscapes of wild and romantic beauty.

DRAKE'S CREEK.
Penn Forest, Carbon Co., Pa.
134 *m. fr. N.Y. Fr. Wilkesbarre,* **42.**

A wild mountain brook here enters

the Lehigh through a deep reft in the hills. At the station is a saw-mill and a few dwellings.

STONY CREEK.
Penn Forest, Carbon Co., Pa.
132 *m.fr.N.Y. Fr.Wilkesbarre,***44.**

Here also is another wild and rocky ravine, with its mountain stream seeking the Lehigh. The river here makes an abrupt turn westward.

PENN HAVEN JUNCTION.
Lausanne, Carbon Co., Pa.
128 *m. fr.N.Y. Fr. Wilkesbarre,***48.**

This is the junction of the Lehigh Valley Railway with the Lehigh and Mahanoy Railway, which now forms a part of the Lehigh Valley Railroad, having been consolidated with it. Here also the Hazleton Railroad Company have a separate road to the top of the mountain opposite, 430 feet high, from which the coal-cars are let down by inclined planes on the other side, a distance of 1200 feet, to the Lehigh River, where the coal is transferred to boats and cars of the Lehigh Valley Railroad These planes are in full view as we approach and leave Penn Haven. Here also the Quakake Creek empties into the Lehigh. The Lehigh Valley Railroad now crosses to the west side. Passing on, the wild mountains are wilder and more picturesque, and so winding is the river that, in looking ahead, no outlet for it through the mountains is visible or seems possible. Steep cliffs and rocky ramparts rise to towering heights above us. Soon again we recross to the east side of the Lehigh by a fine iron bridge, in near view of the tunnel of the Lehigh and Susquehanna Railroad, which also crosses the river to its west side. A short distance below these bridges are a number of large coal-shutes, where canal-boats are loaded and go east.

MAUCH CHUNK,
Mauch Chunk, Carbon Co., Pa.,
121 *m. fr.N.Y. Fr. Wilkesbarre,***55,**

The capital of Carbon county, on the right bank of the Lehigh, at the mouth of Mauch Chunk Creek, is situated in one of the most romantic, picturesque, and wild localities in the United States. It is built in a narrow ravine through which the river passes, where there is but little room for buildings, to say nothing of gardens, surrounded on all sides by rugged mountain spurs, rising precipitously from 800 to 1000 feet in height. Its name is an Indian one, signifying "Bear Mountain."

Susquehanna street, running parallel with the river, and Race street, joining it at right angles, are the principal thoroughfares, upon which stand a number of fine stores and residences, 3 churches, and several hotels.

Although the coal and lumber trade constitutes the chief business of Mauch Chunk, it has 2 foundries and machine-shops, 2 iron forges, a wire and wire-rope manufactory, and a steam flour-mill. Besides these, there are the machine and repair shops of the Lehigh Coal and Navigation Company, and the car repair shops of the Lehigh Valley Company. These various establishments, in connection with the immense amount of transportation by rail and canal from this place, render it an active and enterprising borough.

The rich mines of anthracite coal in its vicinity, however, were the first causes of its growth and wealth, and are still constantly contributing to increase its importance.

Previous to 1813 this whole region was a complete wilderness. Although it was known that coal was to be found in the mountains west from here, all attempts to get it to a market seemed impracticable. In 1817 Josiah White and G. F. Hanto made a reconnoissance of the Lehigh River, in order to ascertain the feasibility of this stream as a means of coal transportation.

The result of this visit was that roads were constructed from the mines to the Lehigh, upon which a series of dams were built to aid its navigation. This was the origin of the Lehigh Coal and Navigation Company, with which the early history of Mauch Chunk is identified. In 1832 this Company gave employment to nearly 400 miners, who, with their families, made a population of 2000. After passing through many financial crises, and expending over $2,500,000 in the enterprise, success crowned their efforts.

The celebrity of the Lehigh coal is very extensive, from the fact that it is the hardest anthracite in the world. The bed upon the top of Mauch Chunk Mountain, or Summit Hill, is 53 feet in thickness, exceeding in this respect, also, any known layer or vein. It covers a large area extending southwest for several miles. In many places it crops out from the hillsides, so as to be easily worked. The road by which the coal is brought down to Mauch Chunk, and the traveler carried up to visit these mines is called the

SWITCH BACK RAILWAY.

Starting from the *"Mansion House,"* where stages leave 3 times a day for the *Switch Back*, we proceed through Susquehanna and Race streets, up a steep ascent, to an elevated plateau, upon which stands what is called Upper Mauch Chunk, 215 feet above the river, and near the foot of the great plane on Mount Pisgah. Here the method by which the cars ascend these planes will attract attention. A railway being constructed with unusual care and strength up the steep mountain-side, the next thing to be accomplished is to construct a perfectly safe, speedy, and easy arrangement for drawing cars up the acclivity. Let us stand and watch the operation of the machinery for this purpose, before risking ourselves upon such an apparently hazardous journey.

Standing at the depot at the foot of the plane, the conductor signals to the engineer at the top, when we first notice a singular-looking vehicle, called a safety-car, emerging from a covered pit beneath us, and coming up in the rear of, and into contact with, the cars which are to be drawn to the summit. The object of lowering the safety-car into this pit is that it may be placed in the rear of the passenger cars, for it is in this that the safety of the arrangement consists. The safety-car is so-called because it has attached to it, on each side, ratchets, which glide over a set of spurs or cogs upon the side of the rails, and which, in case of a breakage of the hoisting band, would prevent its descending the plane by stopping it at once. There are two of these safety-cars, one of which *descends* while the other *ascends*. Attached to the safety-cars are 2 iron bands, 6½ inches wide and 3-16ths of an inch thick, which wind about a drum-wheel, 28 feet in diameter, in the engine-house, and pass over a set of rollers along the plane. The strength of these bands alone sustains the weight of the train. So perfect is the whole machinery connected with this railway that during 20 years not a single passenger has been injured. Let us, then, fear not to take a ride over this unique railway.

Seating ourselves in a covered car, about one-fourth the size of an ordinary railroad car, the conductor pulls the signal-wire, the safety-car emerges from the pit behind us, and we commence the ascent. At first a sensation of timidity will perhaps come over the mind; yet such thoughts are soon dispelled in the sublimity of the prospect that is becoming gradually spread out before us. In six or seven minutes we are on the summit of Mount Pisgah, about 700 feet higher than the foot of the plane, a height we have gained in being drawn up the distance of 2340 feet. Here we are allowed five or ten minutes to survey a scene which it is impossible to describe.

From this lofty eyrie we see at our feet Mauch Chunk, nestling beneath the shadows of the mountains, with the Lehigh River winding its way at their base, now between artificial barriers of masonry, and then pursuing its natural course along its rocky bed, till it is lost to our sight behind the mountain ridges which rise, range after range, about us. Twelve miles distant, toward the south-east, is the Lehigh Water Gap, the magnificent gate in the Blue Ridge which bounds the horizon on the south, and through which the Lehigh makes its way into the unseen valleys beyond.

The pleasing contrasts of light and shadow, verdant foliage, and rugged cliffs, with the silvery river flowing calmly between, is matchless in its loveliness and wild grandeur. No language is too extravagant to utter its praises or to speak the admiration of the beholder.

The railroad from Mount Pisgah to Summit Hill was the first railroad ever constructed in the United States.

Formerly what is now the return railway (not the one we are now on) was a turnpike, over which the coal was brought down to the Lehigh in wagons drawn by two horses. This turnpike, in 1827, under the superintendence of Josiah White, was converted into a railway, on which cars loaded with coal descended by their own gravity to the landing, and, after being emptied, were drawn back by mules. It was the firm conviction of Mr. White, and one which he lived to see realized, that these cars might be made to descend back again to the mines by gravitation, in the same way that they descended to Mauch Chunk. Such a unique contrivance in a back track, called the *switch-back*, he at length originated, which is regarded as a masterpiece of bold and successful engineering, and was completed in 1845.

The method of its operation we explain as we proceed. Mount Pisgah, upon whose eastern end we have ascended, is a portion of a long ridge, extending for many miles toward the west, and forming the southern boundary of the most southerly of the great anthracite coal basins. It is called Sharp Mountain throughout almost its entire extent, on account of the sharp edge which its summit usually presents, being generally made up of perpendicular strata of bare rock. The numerous Appalachian ridges were evidently raised to their present position by some force that was *continental* in its action as well as very regular. It was a crowding or lateral force, tending to make the strata take up less room horizontally. Push against the two sides of a quire of paper or a magazine resting upon a flat surface, and we see that it rises into ridges; and so, if we suppose the interior of the earth to have shrunk away from its former size, no matter how little, its crust, borne down by its own enormous weight, will fit itself to its contents, even though by so doing it is obliged to create *wrinkles* upon the crust. These wrinkles in this region are long and continuous, and range a little south of west.

Having taken as good a view from Mount Pisgah as the time will permit, of the grand scenery it presents, including some of these parallel ridges, we again enter the cars and begin to descend, by the simple force of gravity, along the south slope of the mountain ridge toward the west, at the rate of from ten to fifteen miles an hour.

The scenery throughout the entire length of this descent is varied and pleasing. Shady forest-trees line most of the way, through openings in which we get occasional views of the valley below us on the south. Six miles from the first inclined plane we come to the second, called Mount Jefferson, having lost one half of the ascent of Mount Pisgah. To the top of this plane we are again drawn by a stationary engine in a manner similar to our ascent of the first plane, and, after a shorter second descent, we reach Summit Village, to the north of which lie the numerous Collieries of Panther Creek.

At this village are a number of stores, two hotels, a church, and some pleasant residences. In order, now, to make the circuit of the mines and return back again to Summit, the line of direction is frequently changed, and is somewhat zigzag in its course, accommodating itself to the nature of the ground.

The contrivance for changing the direction of the car at every angle of this zigzag course is called a *switch-back*. The car, by the impetus gained in descending a certain slope, moves a little way up an incline and comes to a standstill. The car then descends to the foot of this incline, and in so doing gains an impetus for ascending another incline, on to which it is moved by a self-regulating *switch*, and this is what is called being *switched back*.

Having descended to the valley of the Panther Creek, we come to the village of COALDALE, in the midst of the Lehigh Coal Company's Mines. This village contains a church and quite a large number of dwellings, inhabited chiefly by miners. The coal here is mined chiefly from the surface, as in a quarry. Through some accident one of the collieries took fire several years since, and is still burning. Much labor and money have been expended to extinguish it, but with no success. The smoke coming up through the ground can be seen as we pass on from Summit Hill.

Having now passed from the top of Mount Pisgah to the valley between it and the Nesquehoning Mountain north of it, we are again drawn up two inclined planes, and then descend back to Mauch Chunk on the southern slope of the ridge, crossing the track by which we came at about half the distance. This ride, throughout its whole extent, is exceedingly pleasant, constantly presenting a variety of novel and romantic scenery. It is nearly 25 miles in extent, and occupies about three hours.

Although this is the crowning object of interest to the tourist to this locality, there are *other* points which are deserving notice.

About three miles north of Mauch Chunk are MOER'S FALLS, on Moer's Creek, near what is called the " *Turn Hole* " in the Lehigh River. These falls are three in number, the first or lowest being 40 feet, the second 70, and the third 35 feet in height.

Prospect Rock, almost directly south of the " *Mansion House*," is a narrow and jutting cliff, easily accessible, though from 200 to 300 feet above the river. From it the view is superb, and one which every visitor should see. In passing through the village the handsome residence of *Judge Packer* will attract attention. It stands a little distance up the mountain-side, overlooking the town and river. The elegant grounds around it were laid out by a Parisian refugee, the head gardener of Louis Philippe, who has transformed the rugged hill slope into a rich garden, with beautiful walks and terraces.

The "MANSION HOUSE," *E. T. Booth, Proprietor*, is located directly opposite the Lehigh and Coal Navigation Company's Railroad Station, and also opposite the station of the Lehigh Valley Railroad, upon the other side of the river, where an omnibus is always in waiting for the accommodation of tourists. It is a commodious five-story building, at the very base of the grand mountains which rise more than 800 feet above and around it. The view from the veranda of this hotel is exceedingly fine. Here the Lehigh makes an abrupt curve eastward, the whole grand sweep of which is in view from the hotel, while its cool and shaded position renders it a delightful summer resort. The Lehigh Coal and Navigation Coal Company are the owners of this hotel, and in its accommodating furniture and appointments it is not inferior to the leading hotels of the metropolis.

LEHIGHTON.

Mahoning, Carbon Co.
117 *m. fr. N. Y. Fr. Wilkesbarre,* **59.**

Just after leaving Mauch Chunk, we cross the Lehigh, and our course then follows the west bank of the river, through a less wild region, passing out of the coal measures entirely, through a slate tract.

Lehighton is a small village, just above the junction of the Mahoning Creek with the Lehigh. The Old Moravian grave-yard, on the hill north, is an object of considerable interest, and commands a fine view of the Mahoning Valley. At the foot of the hill is the site of Gnadenhutten, where twelve of the early settlers were massacred by the Indians in 1775. Their remains are buried in the old cemetery. The Lehigh and Susquehanna Railroad here crosses the river.

Opposite is WEISSPORT, on the left bank of the river. Originally this whole section was occupied by Moravians. At Weissport is an extensive Rolling Mill. Fort Allen Hotel rests upon the site of old Fort Allen, which was built by Benjamin Franklin. This neighborhood was once the scene of Brainerd's missionary labors with the Indians.

PARRYVILLE.
Franklin, Carbon Co., Pa.
115 *m. fr. N. Y. Fr. Wilkesbarre,* **61.**

Here are the smoking furnaces of the Carbon Iron Company, on the other side of the river. A little below, near the Gap, the Lawrence Metallic Paint and Mining Company are erecting a very large establishment for the manufacture of their new fire-proof paint, which is said to be superior in many respects to white lead. The mines from which the paint is obtained, produce eleven different colors, said to be equal in quality to those that are imported.

LEHIGH GAP.
Washington, Lehigh Co., Pa.
110 *m. fr. N. Y. Fr. Wilkesbarre,* **66.**

Here we pass over Lizard Creek, upon which are several mills. At the Gap is a hotel and a number of dwellings. This creek opens a way for the Lehigh River through Blue Mountain, the broken ends of which front upon the river as we pass on for some miles. The best view of the Gap is obtained from the rear car, soon after passing the station, through which, in the distance, we get a narrow glimpse of the Lehigh Mountains. Opposite this station a chain bridge crosses the river.

SLATINGTON.
Washington, Lehigh Co., Pa.
108 *m. fr. N. Y. Fr. Wilkesbarre,* **68.**
HOTELS—*Slatington* and *Railroad Hotel.*

Is a pleasant village, occupied chiefly by Welsh, who are employed in the extensive quarries and manufactories of the *Lehigh Slate* company. These are the pioneer slate works of Pennsylvania. This is probably the most extensive slate region in the world. The Capitol at Washington has been roofed with slate from these quarries, half an inch in thickness. The village is a quarter of a mile west from the station, in a beautiful locality, and has usually quite a number of summer visitors. Near the depot is the American School Slate and Mantel Manufactory. Some of the slate quarries will be seen on the right of the track, as we leave the station.

ROCKDALE.
Washington, Lehigh Co., Pa.
104 *m. fr. N. Y. Fr. Wilkesbarre,* **72.**

A small village in the slate region. Here we pass through a cut in a jutting cliff of slate, which furnishes a good idea of this rock formation. Across the river is a beautiful and fertile rolling country.

LAURY'S.
North White Hall, Lehigh Co., Pa.,
101 *m. fr. N. Y. Fr. Wilkesbarre,* **75.**

Has extensive slate quarries and a planing-mill. Large quantities of iron ore are also mined in the neighborhood, for the furnaces along the Lehigh. The soil is fertile, and there are many fine grain fields in this locality.

WHITEHALL.
North White Hall, Lehigh Co., Pa.
99 *m. fr. N. Y. Fr. Wilkesbarre,* **77.**

A small village of little note. Here is Eckert & Co's. manufactory of Hydraulic Cement, which is mined near by, and is of a superior quality. A covered bridge crosses the river at this place.

COPLAY.

North White Hall, Lehigh Co., Pa.
97 *m. fr. N.Y. Fr. Wilkesbarre,* **79.**

Here are the large iron works of the Lehigh Iron Company, so near the railroad that one can feel the heat of their furnaces in passing. Directly below is a foundry and machine-shop.

HOKENDAUQUA.

South White Hall, Lehigh Co., Pa.,
96 *m. fr. N.Y. Fr. Wilkesbarre,* **80.**

Is a pleasant village on the riverbank, where are located Thomas's Iron Works, consisting of four large furnaces, which are among the largest in this country. The Hokendauqua Creek here empties into the Lehigh.

CATASAUQUA.

Hanover, Lehigh Co., Pa.
95 *m. fr. N.Y. Fr. Wilkesbarre,* **81.**

HOTEL—*Pennsylvania Hotel.*

Upon the opposite side of the river is a thriving borough, with a population of about 4000. It contains a number of fine churches, a bank, several hotels, two machine-shops, two rolling-mills, gas works, and five large blast-furnaces, belonging to the Lehigh Crane Company. It is stated that one of these furnaces has turned out 248 tons of iron in a week, a yield scarcely equaled in this or any other country. Its position is in the midst of a rich iron and limestone country, which, with its railroad and canal communications, are highly favorable to its future growth.

The Catasauqua and Fogelsville Railroad, which was built to transport iron ore from the mines, here connects with the Lehigh Valley Railroad. Over 150,000 tons of ore are carried over this road annually. The bridge for this Railway, as well as common travel, crosses the river near the station.

FURNACE,

Allentown, Lehigh Co., Pa.,
93 *m. fr. N.Y. Fr. Wilkesbarre,* **83,**

One mile from Allentown depot, in the northern part of the town, contains the Allentown Furnaces and Rolling-Mills, for the manufacture of Railroad Iron.

ALLENTOWN

Lehigh Co., Pa.
92 m. fr. N.Y. Fr. Harrisburg, 90.

There are two stations for this city, one in its eastern part, near the Lehigh River, and the other at the junction of the Lehigh Valley and East Pennsylvania Railroads.

The city is one of the handsomest in eastern Pennsylvania. Its name is derived from that of its original owner, James Allen, who laid it out in 1762. It is the capital of Lehigh county, and is situated at the junction of the Lehigh River and Jordan Creek, which runs through the northern part of the town. The eminence upon which it is built commands a fine prospect, and slopes gradually to the Lehigh on the east, and the Jordan Creek on the north. The difficulty of obtaining water was, for a time, a hinderance to its growth ; but the town was at length supplied, in 1828, from Norman's Spring, about a mile distant.

The streets are regularly laid out, and lighted with gas by the Allen Gas Company. Main street is the principal thoroughfare.

Public Buildings.

The Court-House is a handsome building of blue limestone, two stories in height, and surmounted by a cupola.

Muhlenberg College is a newly organized institution for boys, introducing a military system in their training. Both of these buildings stand upon Main street, and will attract the attention of visitors.

Allentown has also a theological seminary, a number of fine churches, and several banks and newspaper offices.

Manufactures.

Of late years its industrial interests have been largely developed, contributing much to its prosperity. Among its manufacturing establishments are the *Allentown Iron Co.'s Furnace*, which produces 20,000 tons of pig-iron per annum, for which the ore is mined in the vicinity, near the Lehigh Valley Railroad; *Roberts' Iron Furnace* ; the *Lehigh Valley Rolling-Mill*, for the manufacture of railroad and bar iron, spikes, rivets, etc. ; the *Allentown Rolling-Mill*, making railroad iron ; *Hope Rolling-Mill*, the *Jordan Manufacturing Co.'s Rolling-Mill*, besides other establishments for the manufacture of castings, machinery, gas and steam pipes, boilers, axles, carriages, pianos, files and fire-arms. Nearly all the iron ore used by these mills is obtained a short distance from the East-Pennsylvania Railroad, between Allentown and Bower's Station.

The Lehigh River, a tributary of the Delaware, rises in Luzerne county, near Wilkesbarre, running to Allentown in a south-easterly or nearly southerly course. Here the Lehigh Hills bar its further progress toward the south, and compel it to take an easterly direction. This stream formerly abounded with trout and shad, before dams were erected across it. The landscape is everywhere in this region picturesque and beautiful ; the adjacent country is fertile, and the farms well improved. Extensive beds of iron ore, limestone, and roofing slate are found in the vicinity. Here are mineral springs that are highly prized by those who have tried their efficacy. A visit to " Big Rock," 1000 feet in height, a short distance from the city, will amply repay the tourist.

BETHLEHEM.

Lower Saucon, Northampton Co., Pa.
87 *m. fr. N. Y. Fr. Harrisburg,* **95.**
HOTELS—*Sun, Eagle, Fetter's,* and *Pennsylvania House.*

Bethlehem is one of the oldest Moravian settlements in this country. The Moravians came to the New World early in its history, both to avoid persecution and to attempt the conversion of the Indians to Christianity. They first settled in Georgia, but in 1738 their settlement was broken up, on account of a war then raging between England and Spain, in which the Brethren were compelled to serve, and their attention was directed to Pennsylvania. The strict morality and even severity of their manner of life were far from a hinderance to them in their enterprise. "They held all property in common ; the support of the aged and infirm was made a general concern ; and even the regulation of marriages was a matter in which the individuals directly concerned had less to do than any body else."

The settlement at Bethlehem, made in 1741, was the earliest in Pennsylvania, and retained its original economy longer than any other. The obloquy and contempt which were bestowed upon them by their neighbors, the Germans and Irish, only served to strengthen the bond of union among them.

The separation of the sexes and community of property existed as late as 1762. From that time their distinctive characteristics have more and more ceased to be noticeable.

The old buildings, for the most part, still remain, and are objects of curious interest to the tourist. The principal ones stand in Church row, at the foot of Broad street, near the Sun Hotel. They are built of stone, and appear capable of enduring for many years to come. Here the infirm and aged are still supported by the Brethren as of old.

The old grave-yard of the Moravians is an interesting place to visit. It is in the centre of the town, and is filled with graves of whites, Indians, and negroes, arranged with none of the fastidious discriminations of the present age. The Moravian church is a large stone edifice, 142 feet long, in the Gothic style.

The borough has a pleasant and commanding situation on the north bank of the Lehigh River, is regularly laid out, its streets finely shaded with an abundance of trees, and is a favorite place of resort in summer.

Some historic interest attaches to this place from the fact that Washington, in his retreat across the Delaware, was compelled to remove his hospital and supplies to Bethlehem. The Moravians gave the use of their buildings to the government, which at one time were filled by a large body of British prisoners. Thus the town came to be honored by the presence of Washington, Adams, Lafayette, Pulaski, Gates, Hancock, and Franklin. The "Single Sisters" gave Count Pulaski a banner of crimson silk, embroidered, which is now in the Historical Society's rooms at Baltimore. Longfellow has made this incident the subject of a poem.

MANUFACTURES.

The *Bethlehem Iron Co.'s* works are the finest in this whole valley, which is so celebrated for its extensive iron manufactories. At their rolling-mill large quantities of railroad iron are manufactured.

The *Lehigh Zinc* works are also located here, besides numerous other smaller establishments.

THE LEHIGH UNIVERSITY.

Bethlehem is the site of the *Lehigh University*, which was formally opened on September 1st, 1866. During the year 1865, the Hon. Asa Packer, of Mauch Chunk, announced, unsolicited, to the Bishop of the Diocese, his intention to appropriate the sum of $500,000 and an eligible spot in South-Bethlehem, containing 56 acres, for the purpose of founding an educational institution, which should bear the name of the *Lehigh University*. The purpose of the founder in making this munificent endowment was to provide the means for imparting to young men of the State a complete professional education, which should fit them to take an active part in the practical duties of the time.

The system adopted proposes to introduce those important branches "which have been heretofore more or less neglected in what purports to be a liberal education; and especially those industrial pursuits which tend to develop the resources of the country, such as Engineering, Chemistry, Metallurgy, Architecture, and Construction." The institution is designed to be *polytechnic* in its character, so that the instruction which it imparts will enable its graduates to play intelligent parts in exploring and developing the vast resources of the United States.

Its site is peculiarly adapted for the purposes to which it has been devoted, upon a gentle declivity of the Lehigh Mountain range, in the midst of a park of forest-trees, 365 feet above tide water, having an unobstructed view for twenty miles.

Packer Hall, the principal university building, is a handsome edifice of stone, 213 feet long, standing 700 feet back of Packer avenue, the front limit of the grounds. Near it are erected houses for the President and professors.

Toward the eastern extremity of the grounds stands *Christmas Hall*, a commodious brick edifice, containing a chapel, lecture-rooms, and students' dormitories.

This College had at its opening 40 students, and will, without doubt, become one of the most important and prosperous educational institutions in the country.

The Moravians have here a large female seminary, which has a high reputation throughout Pennsylvania. There are, in this borough, five hotels, four churches, and a newspaper office. The streets are lighted with gas, and the borough is supplied with water from Manockisy Creek.

The railroad station is not within the limits of the borough, which lies entirely north of the river. Quite a village has sprung up on the south side of the river, called *Bethlehem South*, in the township of Lower Saucon. Here is the junction of the North-Pennsylvania Railroad, leading to Philadelphia, and forming its most direct route to the Lehigh Valley.

FREEMANSBURG.

Lower Saucon, Northampton Co., Pa. **84** *m. fr. N.Y. Fr. Harrisburg,* **98.**

A pretty and thriving borough, extending along the opposite or north side of the Lehigh River, in the township of Bethlehem. Here are several quite extensive canal-boat building establishments. The borough contains some two hundred inhabitants, a church, and two hotels. A bridge connects it with the south side of the river.

About two miles north, in Bethlehem township, is the small village of BUTZTOWN, and a little south of the station, in Lower Saucon, is SHIMERSVILLE, another small village on Saucon Creek, containing a woolen factory, a saw-mill, a grist-mill, a store, and a hotel. Here a branch railroad extends across about a mile to the North-Pennsylvania Railroad.

LIME RIDGE.

Lower Saucon, Northampton Co., Pa.
82 *m.fr. N.Y. Fr.Harrisburg,* **100.**

Here are a number of lime-kilns, the stone being supplied by the quarries in the vicinity, and the railroad affording convenient facilities for obtaining coal and for forwarding lime. Much of the lime, however, is used by farmers in the region around for improving the land. The scenery along the Lehigh about here is very beautiful. Just below this station is Smith's Island, in the Lehigh River, covered with shade trees, and a favorite resort for picnics, etc.

Methods of Mining Coal.

There are three methods of mining coal, namely: First, by "*Drifts*," when the coal is above "*water level*," that is, when it lies in upturned or sloping veins in a mountain or high hill. In this case, if the end of the seam of coal can be conveniently reached in some gap in the containing ridge, the drift or "*gangway*" into the coal is cut at the lowest available point from which the water can be drained away without pumping. If no such opportunity is found, but the geological indications prove that the coal is attainable in the hill or mountain, then a horizontal *tunnel* through the rock, about at right angles to the direction of the seam, is cut at a convenient point. This tunnel extends through the rock measures which lie between the coal and the surface, and, when the coal is reached, horizontal gangways are turned in it to the right and left.

All the coal lying *above* these gangways is then accessible, and can be drawn out after being "*mined*," (that is, separated from the seam by blasting,) without lifting or handling it, since it falls by its own weight into the mine wagons, which are drawn in and out along the gangways by mules. The gangways are provided for this purpose with iron railway tracks.

This method of mining is by far the most economical, and, where the location of the seams will admit of it, can be carried on to great advantage in competition with the other methods. All the expensive machinery for pumping out the water and hoisting up the coal is thereby avoided.

Much of the coal in the Lehigh and Schuylkill regions has been mined in that way, and a little in the Lackawanna;

but in all the regions except the Mahanoy nearly all that lies above water level has been obtained, and the other two methods have to be resorted to to get the coal.

The second method of mining is by "*Slopes.*" The seams of coal in the Wyoming and Lackawanna region are somewhat in the form of an immense canoe, underlying the whole region, but coming up to the surface on the sides of the encircling mountains at an angle more or less inclined to the horizon.

At convenient points, where the seams "*crop out*" or come to the surface, inclined passages are cut in the coal itself called "*Slopes.*" These descend to a convenient distance, and then gangways are turned to the right and left, tracks are laid in them, and the coal mined in the same manner as that above described; suitable machinery being erected at the top of the stope for hoisting the mine wagons when filled up the inclined track of the slope, and for pumping out the water which accumulates in the mine.

When all the coal above the gangway is worked out, "another lift is sunk," in the language of the miner; that is, the slope is excavated down another convenient distance, say fifty to one hundred yards, gangways are again turned, and the coal between the two gangways is then mined. When this is worked out, another lift is sunk, and so on until all the coal in the seam is obtained. Pillars are left between the chambers as before; and, when all the chambers or breasts on the property are worked out, the pillars are then removed, or, in technical language, "the mine is robbed" of its supports, and usually the unsupported roof soon after falls in. By carelessness and mismanagement large quantities of coal are frequently shut in by these falls in such a way as to become irretrievably lost, the cost of again reopening being greater than the value of the coal.

The third method of mining is by perpendicular "*Shafts.*"

These are made use of on tracts of coal land where the seams do not come to the surface at all, or rise above any part of it, as it sometimes does in the side of a mountain. A large part of the Lackawanna region is situated in this way. There are seams of coal which do not come to the surface at all, except on the two sides of the lower valley, where the upheaved mountains have lifted them up, and these regions form one broad "*basin*" of coal.

The Schuylkill and Mahanoy regions are each divided into several long, narrow basins, some or all of the seams of which underlie each other, cropping out on the sides of each basin. Some of these basins are very deep, so that shafts through the solid rock would be very expensive. For this reason they are not usually so well adapted to mining in those regions as slopes, drifts, and tunnels.

In the Lackawanna and Wyoming region the coal generally lies almost level at a moderate distance below the surface, and, away from the mountain-sides, is commonly reached by shafts. These are sunk until the coal seam is reached, when gangways are run horizontally in the coal as before. The machinery for hoisting and pumping is at the top of the shaft.

When the wagons on these gangways are filled with coal, they are drawn by mules to the foot of the shaft, and then hoisted by steam power to the surface or to the hopper of the breaker.

The coal is now in large, irregular lumps, mixed with a considerable quantity of slate rock in large and small fragments, finely powdered coal, dirt, etc. Workmen stand ready with picks to break up any pieces too large to go into the breaker, and to throw out the large fragments of rock.

The *breaker* consists of two large iron rollers with toothed surfaces, between which the coal passes and is crushed or cracked into fragments of various sizes. After passing between these rollers, it is emptied into large cylindrical revolving *screens* made of iron wire or bars, woven together in such a way as to form meshes of different dimensions. The screens are inclined somewhat from a horizontal position, so that the larger meshes are at the lower end. The fine dirt passes out first near the top, then the small sizes of coal known as pea coal, nut coal, etc., and so on up to the largest lump coal, which passes out at the lower end of the screen.

Each size is dropped from the screen into a separate shute, along which sit small boys, who pick out the slate stone, which is always more or less mixed with the pure coaL The shutes are so inclined that the coal slides into bins over the railroad track, from which the coal is let into the cars, which are placed directly underneath for that purpose. It will be seen that by these arrangements the coal is not handled or lifted at all ; a very convenient arrangement, and one by which the price of coal is made very much lower than it would otherwise be.

The miners are paid a stipulated sum per wagon-load drawn from the mine, and commonly earn from three to six dollars per day.

It is seldom that accidents happen in the mines, and when they do it is usually owing to the carelessness of the miners themselves, who sometimes enter dangerous places without a properly protected light, and the *fire-damp*, or "*sulphur*," as the miners ignorantly call it, takes fire, with a violent explosion. Insufficient pillars or props sometimes occasion a fall of the roof of a chamber or gangway ; but some premonition is usually given, so that escape is easily made before the wall breaks in.

We can not fail to see a wise provision in the storing up within the earth these vast resources for man's present and future wants. Yet it is quite probable that, notwithstanding the apparently inexhaustible amount of fuel contained in the anthracite coal measures of Eastern Pennsylvania, one or two centuries may so diminish the available portions of them as to necessitate the transportation of the bituminous coal of the West to the Eastern States, or its importation from Nova Scotia or elsewhere.

There is a great difference between the modes of mining anthracite and bituminous coals, owing to the geological positions of the different kinds of coal.

The bituminous coal is spread over very large areas in several of the Western and Southern States, including Western Pennsylvania, Ohio, West-Virginia, Illinois, Iowa, Missouri, Alabama, Tennessee, etc. Also in Nova Scotia, New-Brunswick, and Newfoundland.

It usually lies in flat, nearly horizontal seams, the originally horizontal stratifications of the rocks having been but little disturbed.

These seams occur, one above another, between layers of solid sandstone and slate rock, at distances from each other varying from a thin seam of slate up to several hundred feet of alternating slate and sandstone. The thickness of the coal seams varies from a few inches up to twenty feet, or even more in rare cases.

The most available of these seams for working are where streams of running water have in the long course of ages worn out valleys, like those of the Alleghany and Ohio Rivers and their tributaries. Here the coal is seen on the sides of the valleys in its original position between the rocks, and is worked in horizontal excavations, leaving pillars to support the walls of the various chambers and galleries. In other places, where deep river valleys do not afford such a convenient mode of access to the coal, perpendicular shafts have to be sunk to the different seams.

While the entire area of territory under which bituminous coal is found in the United States is estimated at over one hundred and thirty thousand square miles, the anthracite only occupies a little over four hundred square miles.

The anthracite coal of Pennsylvania lies wholly between the nearly parallel ridges of the great Appalachian system of mountains, a region which indicates great geological disturbance. Whether, at the time these remarkable ridges were uplifted, a great subterranean heat operated to drive out all the volatile matter associated with the coal, thus converting what was once bituminous into anthracite coal, at the same time that the strata containing it were upheaved into the form of long, narrow, parallel basins as now found, is a matter for the geologist to determine.

FLORENCE SEWING-MACHINES.

FOSTER & RICHARDSON,

(Successors to C. PATCH & CO.,) General Agts. for New England, New York, & New Jersey,

Office of the Nonotuck & Union Silk Companies,

505 Broadway, New York.   141 Washington St., Boston.

Florence Sewing-Machine.

All parties in want of a good Sewing-Machine for family use, or cloth work of any kind, will please examine the FLORENCE before purchasing elsewhere.

We claim that the FLORENCE is an improvement over all others. The stitch is more elastic, alike on both sides of the fabric, almost noiseless, simple in construction, is not liable to get out of repair. Having a reversible feed, enabling the operator to stitch either to the left or right at pleasure, making four different stitches —lock, knot, double-lock, and double-knot. Easy to operate, and will do a larger range of work than can be done by any other sewing-machine. The FLORENCE MACHINE is licensed, and parties purchasing of us or our agents need not have any doubts in regard to using them. All machines sold are warranted in every particular, and kept in repair one year free of charge; and any one purchasing of us, and not satisfied, can return them by allowing five dollars per month for the use of them.

Machine-Needles of all kinds, Shuttles, Bobbins, Oil, Silk, Cotton and Machine Trimmings, etc., constantly on hand.

Agents for the sale of the *Bickford Family Knitting-Machine,* an improvement over all others. Price, $30. Liberal discount to the Trade.

FOSTER & RICHARDSON, General Agents,
505 Broadway, New York.   141 Washington St., Boston.

The Celebrated Imitation Gold
$15 Hunting Watches. $20
THE COLLINS OROIDE WATCH FACTORY.

CASES
OF THE
COLLINS METAL
(Improved Oroide.)

SPECIAL NOTICE.—Our superior Oroide Watches having recently been imitated, and worthless Watches sold in New York, Boston, Chicago, and other cities, represented as our Watches, we hereby caution the public against them, and give notice that we are in no way responsible for these bogus concerns, and only those purchasing directly from us can secure a genuine Watch of our manufacture. We have recently greatly improved our Oroide in appearance and durability, and to protect the public from imposition hereafter, have named it the "COLLINS METAL," and we give notice that any one making use of this name will be prosecuted to the extent of the law.

This metal has all the brilliancy and durability of Gold; can not be distinguished from it by the best judges; retains its color till worn out, and is equal to Gold excepting in intrinsic value. All our Gentlemen's Watches are *Full-Jeweled Patent Levers;* those for Ladies an improved Escapement, better than a Lever for a small Watch; all in Hunting-Cases, and fully guaranteed by special certificate. The $15 Watches are equal in neatness, style of finish, general appearance, and for time, to Gold one costing $150. Those for $20 are of extra fine finish, and are fully equal to a Gold Watch costing $200. Chains of every style, from $2 to $6. Also, Jewelry of the Collins Metal in every style.

TO CLUBS.—Where Six Watches are ordered at one time we will send one extra Watch free of charge.

Goods sent to any part of the United States by express, to be paid for on delivery. Money need not be sent with the order, as bills can be paid when goods are taken from the express office. Customers must pay all express charges. We employ no Agents; orders must therefore be sent directly to us. Customers in the city will remember that our *only Office* is

Nos. 37 & 39 Nassau St., New York, Opp. the Post-Office (Upstairs).
C. E. COLLINS & CO.

No. 13 Laight St., New York.
Opposite 395 Canal Street.
Reopened, Renovated, Improved!!

THIS CELEBRATED BATH, so long and favorably known throughout the country after a thorough renovation and various improvements, is again open to the public.

IF YOU WISH TO ENJOY A RARE LUXURY;

If you wish to be cleaner than you ever was before; if you wish to have a healthy, active, beautiful skin; if you wish to purify your blood; if you wish to rid yourself of Colds, Rheumatism, Neuralgia, etc.; if you wish to preserve your health; if you wish to gratify your curiosity;

TRY A TURKISH BATH!
You will be sure to like it and to come again.

BATHING HOURS:
Gentlemen......6 to 8 A. M., 1 to 9 P. M. | Ladies............... 10 to 12 A. M
SUNDAYS—Gents........6 to 12 A. M.

Parties can be accommodated with Good Hygienic Board and Rooms at the Turkish Bath Institute. Also with ELECTRIC BATHS, SWEDISH MOVEMENT CURE, &c.

Traders' Express Company.

GENERAL OFFICE:
8 Park Place, New York.

DRAFTS AND BILLS COLLECTED,

MONEY, PACKAGES, and FREIGHT

Forwarded to all the principal Stations on the line of the

MORRIS AND ESSEX RAILWAY

And connecting with all the responsible Express Companies in New York to all parts of the Country.

Branch Offices in New York:
114 READE STREET,
88 FRANKLIN STREET,
66 CORTLANDT STREET,
and 117 JOHN STREET.

Offices in Newark, N. J.:
MORRIS AND ESSEX DEPOT,
and 134 MARKET STREET.

Freight taken to the following Stations, via.

MORRIS & ESSEX & SUSSEX RAILROADS.

Andover,	*Drakesville,*	*Newton,*	*Stanhope,*
Broadway,	EASTON, Pa.	NEWARK,	*Stanley,*
Boonton,	*Hackettstown,*	*Orange,*	*Stewartsville,*
Bloomfield,	*Morristown,*	*Philipsburgh,*	*Summit,*
Chatham,	*Madison,*	*Rockaway,*	*Waterloo,*
Danville,	MONT CLAIR,	*South Orange,*	*Washington.*
Dover,	*Millburn,*		

And to *ALL STATIONS* and *VILLAGES* on or near the line of the above-named *Railways*.

IRA BUDD,
President.
C. W. POMEROY,
Gen'l Superintendent.

SAMUEL L. BUCK,
Secretary and Treasurer.
A. G. DICKINSON,
Gen'l Manager.

W. A. WILLARD & CO.

MANUFACTURERS

OF

Looking-Glasses,

177 Canal St., NEW YORK,

177 Canal St., NEW YORK,

2d BLOCK WEST OF BOWERY.

Having largely increased our facilities for manufacturing LOOKING-GLASSES, &c., we are prepared to offer to the public goods in our line of superior quality, at the

LOWEST PRICES,

Both to the Wholesale and Retail Trade. We have on hand at all times a very large stock of

PIER AND MANTEL MIRRORS,

BASE AND TRIPOD TABLES,

Cornices,

Marble Slabs, and Brackets, &c.

Hotels and Private Houses Fitted at short notice.

Please give us a call, and examine Goods.

W. A. WILLARD & CO.,
177 Canal Street, New York.

DELAWARE, LACKAWANNA & WESTERN R.R.— MORRIS & ESSEX RAILROAD.

Depots in New York, foot of Barclay street and foot of Christopher street.

Time Table. May 10th, 1869.

FROM NEW YORK.				STATIONS.	TO NEW YORK.			
Scrant'n Express.	H'k'lst'n Mail.	Le Val'y Express.	Through Mail.		H'k'lst'n Mail.	Le Val'y Express.	Through Mail.	Scrant'n Express.
P.M.	P.M.	A.M.	A.M.	LEAVE ARRIVE	A.M.	A.M.	P.M.	P.M.
4 00	3 30	11 30	8 00	N. York, ft. Barclay st.	9 35	10 30	4 55	9 40
4 15	3 45	11 45	8 15	Hoboken	9 25	10 20	4 45	9 25
4 40	4 10	12 10	8 40	Newark	9 00	9 55	4 20	9 00
....	....	....	....	Roseville	....	....	....	....
....	....	....	....	East Orange	....	....	....	....
....	....	....	....	Orange Junction	....	....	....	....
....	....	....	....	Brick Church	....	....	....	....
....	....	....	8 52	Orange	....	....	4 08	8 50
....	....	....	....	Orange Valley	....	....	....	....
....	....	....	....	Montrose	....	....	....	....
....	....	....	8 58	South Orange	....	....	4 02	....
....	....	....	....	Maplewood	....	....	....	....
....	4 39	....	9 06	Millburn	8 36	....	3 54	8 36
....	4 48	....	9 16	Summit	8 27	....	3 45	8 27
....	....	....	....	New Providence	....	....	....	....
....	4 56	....	9 24	Chatham	8 17	....	3 36	....
5 23	5 02	....	9 30	Madison	8 10	9 13	3 30	8 12
....	....	....	....	Convent	....	....	....	....
5 33	5 13	....	9 45	Morristown	8 00	9 05	3 20	8 00
....	5 20	....	9 51	Morris Plains	7 52	....	3 13	....
....	5 30	....	10 00	Denville	7 40	....	3 01	....
....	6 00	....	10 30	Boonton	7 15	....	2 40	....
....	5 35	....	10 05	Rockaway	7 35	....	2 56	....
6 00	5 45	1 40	10 15	Dover	7 27	8 35	2 46	7 30
6 50	6 50	....	10 55	Succasunna	....	7 56	....	....
7 15	7 15	....	11 15	Chester	....	7 30	....	....
....	5 59	....	10 27	Drakesville	7 14	....	2 32	7 16
....	6 09	....	10 38	Stanhope	7 04	....	2 20	7 05
6 31	6 17	....	10 45	Waterloo	6 57	....	2 13	6 57
6 50	6 50	....	....	Andover	6 40	....	1 45	5 45
7 00	7 00	....	....	Newton	6 30	....	1 30	5 30
6 42	6 30	2 25	10 58	Hackettstown	6 45	7 53	1 58	6 45
6 54	....	....	11 12	Port Murray	....	7 41	1 40	6 26
7 02	....	2 46	11 20	Washington	....	7 33	1 30	6 15
8 13	....	....	12 45	Water Gap	....	....	12 00	5 16
8 25	....	....	1 00	Stroudsburg	....	....	12 46	5 06
10 35	....	....	3 45	Scranton	....	....	9 15	2 55
7 13	....	....	11 31	Broadway	....	7 23	1 17	5 59
7 23	....	....	11 40	Stewartsville	....	7 14	1 05	5 47
7 32	....	3 17	11 50	Phillipsburg	....	7 05	12 53	5 35
7 35	....	3 20	11 52	Easton	....	7.00	12 50	5 30
P.M.	P.M.	A.M	A.M.	ARRIVE LEAVE	A.M.	A.M.	P.M.	P.M.

[MORRIS & ESSEX.]

MORRIS & ESSEX R. R. TIME TABLE—*Continued.*

MORRIS & ESSEX RAILROAD LOCAL TRAINS.

	Start from New York.	*Start for New York.*
MORRISTOWN Trains.	8.00, 11.30, 11.40 A.M.; 3.00, 3.30, 4.00, 5.10, 6.30 P.M.	6.30, 7.05, 8.00, 9.05 A.M.; 12.45, 3.20, 4.30, 8.00 P.M.
SUMMIT Trains.	6.30, 8.00, 11.40 A.M.; 3.00, 3.30, 4.30, 5.10, 6.30 P.M.	6.15, 6.55, 7.26, 8.27, 8.40 A.M.; 1.15, 3.45, 5.00, 8.27 P.M.
SOUTH ORANGE Trains.	6.30, 7.30, 9.30, 11.40 A.M.; 1.00, 3.00, 3.40, 4.30, 5.10, 5.30, 6.30, 8.45, 11.45 P.M.	6.36, 7.10, 7.44, 8.00, 9.00, 10.05 A.M.; 12.05, 1.37, 3.05, 4.02, 4.15, 5.21, 6.35, 7.00, 10.35 P.M.
NEWARK Trains.	6.30, 7.30, 8.30, 9.30, 10.20, 11.00, 11.30, 11.40 A.M.; 1.00, 2.00, 3.00, 3.30, 3.40, 3.50, 4.00, 4.30, 5.00, 5.10, 5.30, 6.10, 6.30, 7.45, 8.45, 11.45 P.M.	6.00, 7.00, 7.35, 7.50, 8.00, 8.30, 8.45, 9.00, 9.25, 9.55, 10.30, 11.00, 11.30 A.M.; 12.30, 1.30, 2.00, 3.30, 4.00, 4.20, 4.40, 5.30, 5.45, 7.00, 9.00, 11.00 P.M.
MONTCLAIR. New'k & Bl'mf'd R.R	8.30, 11.00 A.M.; 2.00, 3.50, 5.00, 6.10 P.M.	6.30, 7.30, 8.25, 10.35 A.M.; 1.05, 3.35, 5.10, 6.30 P.M.

CONNECTIONS.

At *Newark* with Newark & Bloomfield Railroad for Bloomfield, Montclair, etc.

At *Denville* with Boonton Branch for Boonton.

At *Dover* with Chester R. R. for Succasunna and Chester.

At *Waterloo* with Sussex Railroad for Andover and Newton.

At *Washington* with Del., Lack. & W. R. R. for Water Gap, Stroudsburg, Scranton, and Great Bend.

At *Phillipsburg* with Belvidere Delaware Railroad for Belvidere, etc.

At *Easton* with Lehigh Valley Railroad for Bethlehem, Allentown, Mauch Chunk, and also with Lehigh and Susquehanna Railroad for Mauch Chunk, Wilkesbarre and Scranton, and all points in the Pennsylvania coal regions.

The train leaving New York at **8.00 a.m.** and **4.00 p.m.** connects at Washington with the Delaware, Lackawanna and Western Railroad for Water Gap, Stroudsburg, Scranton, and points on the Lackawanna and Bloomsburg Railroad.

The train leaving New York at **11.30 a.m.** connects at Easton with Lehigh Valley Railroad for Bethlehem, Allentown, and Mauch Chunk; also at Washington with Delaware, Lackawanna and Western Railroad for Water Gap, Stroudsburg, and Scranton.

The Through Mail leaving New York at **8.00 a.m.** connects with Lehigh and S. R.R. for all stations on that road.

THE STEAM FIRE-PROOF SAFE,

SANBORN'S PATENT.

THE BEST SAFE IN THE WORLD

PERFECTLY DRY IN USE—ACTUALLY FIRE-PROOF.

It has been more severely tried than any other, and never failed.

The special excellence of this Safe consists in a lining of copper vessels containing water between the bookcase and the walls, whereby, in case of fire, steam is generated, which carries out the heat as it comes in; and thus protects the contents through the longest and severest fires that ever occur. It is thoroughly made, and furnished with the best burglar-proof lock.

The vessels are sealed, so that the water cannot evaporate to dampen the Safe. The solder that closes the opening melts below boiling heat, to let off the steam. "Return Pipes" prevent the water from escaping, in case the Safe over turns when burning. It is entirely dry in use; never needs a new supply of water is very strong, and will resist several times as much fire as ordinary Safes.

All persons needing Fire-proof Safes should send for a pamphlet, and learn all about the STEAM SAFE, before purchasing.

Perfectly satisfactory information furnished to all inquirers.

OVER EIGHTY SAFES FAILED IN ONE FIRE IN PORTLAND.
MORE OR LESS OF THE ORDINARY SAFES FAIL IN NEARLY EVERY SEVERE FIRE.
THE STEAM SAFE NEVER FAILED.
No Valuables Entrusted to it were ever Lost.

WHAT IS SAID OF IT.

"The fire-proof quality of the Steam Improvement is established beyond question; and since so many safes, in recent great fires, have failed to preserve their contents, an improvement like this must be welcomed with great satisfaction."—*Boston Daily Advertiser.*

"An absolutely FIRE-PROOF Safe is at last before the public."—*Philadelphia Press, Sept. 21, 1867.*

"The trial of Steam Fire-Proof Safes, at the Inter-State Fair, gave the greatest possible satisfaction, and further demonstrated their superiority over all others. They are being fully appreciated now by our mercantile community, and we take great pleasure in calling attention to them."—*Philadelphia Inquirer, Sept. 20, 1867.*

"Sanborn's invention has been proved by the most satisfactory tests to be exactly what its manufacturers represent."—*Portland Daily Press, March 3, 1868.*

"These safes are rapidly superseding every other kind, and in their improved form are superior to every other."—*Boston Daily Evening Traveller.*

Manufactured and Sold by

AMERICAN STEAM FIRE-PROOF SAFE COMPANY.

NEW YORK, 300 Broadway.
BOSTON, 60 Sudbury Street.
BALTIMORE, 28 South Street.

HEARTH AND HOME,

AN ILLUSTRATED WEEKLY OF SIXTEEN HANDSOME FOLIO PAGES, FOR THE

FARM, GARDEN, and FIRESIDE.

EDITED BY

DONALD G. MITCHELL and HARRIET BEECHER STOWE,

assisted by a corps of able editors and contributors in all departments. It contains every week original articles by the best American Writers, each in his own department, on

FARMING,   *RURAL ARCHITECTURE,*
GARDENING,   *FRUIT GROWING,*
FLOWER CULTURE, etc.

It also contains Adventures by Sea and Land, Pure and Elevating Stories, Sketches, Biographies, Poems, etc.

Mrs. STOWE, GRACE GREENWOOD, Mrs. MARY E. DODGE, contribute regularly, and the best writers in the country will constantly enrich its pages.

Terms for 1869.

Single Copies $4, invariably in advance; 3 Copies $10; 5 Copies $15. Any one sending us $24 for a club of 8 Copies (all at one time), will receive a copy free.

PETTENGILL, BATES & CO.,

37 Park Row, New York.

PARK HOTEL,

ON THE

American Plan.

CORNER OF

Beekman and Nassau Sts.,

(Near City Hall Park,)   NEW YORK.

GEORGE WIGHT, Proprietor.

N. B.—Located in the very heart of the Wholesale Business, this is one of the most conveniently located Hotels for Merchants, Business Men and others, visiting this City.

NEW YORK TO MONTREAL AND THE WHITE MOUNTAINS.

TO MONTREAL,
VIA
NEW LONDON, BRATTLEBORO', BELLOWS FALLS, RUTLAND, BURLINGTON, AND PLATTSBURG.

TO WHITE MOUNTAINS,
VIA
NEW LONDON, BRATTLEBORO', BELLOWS FALLS, WHITE RIVER JUNCTION, WELLS RIVER, AND LITTLETON.

STATIONS.	Mls.	P.M.		STATIONS.	Mls.	P.M.	
New York...Leave.	0	5 00	P.M.	Montreal.....Leave.	0	5 00	A.M.
New London.......	126	5 00	A.M.	Mooers Junction...	43	6 57	"
Norwich	139	5 35	"	Plattsburg.........	63	7 50	"
Palmer......... {ar. lv.	192	7 45 / 8 05	"	Burlington	87	9 30	"
Amherst...........	212	9 00	"	Rutland....... {ar. lv.	155	12 15 / 12 20	P.M.
Grout's Corner. {ar. lv.	227	9 35 / 9 40	"	Bellows Falls. {ar. lv.	207	2 30 / 2 35	"
South Vernon......	238	10 10	"	Brattleboro'... {ar. lv.	231	3 20 / 3 25	"
Brattleboro'... {ar. lv.	248	10 35 / 10 40	"	South Vernon......	241	3 50	"
Bellows Falls. {ar. lv.	272	11 35 / 11 40	"	Grout's Corner...lv.	252	4 20	"
Rutland....... {ar. lv.	324	2 00 / 2 05	P.M.	Amherst............	267	4 58	"
Burlington.........	392	4 35	"	Palmer......... {ar. lv.	287	5 50 / 6 15	"
Plattsburg.........	416	7 00	"	Norwich...........	340	8 47	"
Mooers Junction...	436	7 53	"	New London.......	353	9 23	"
Montreal	479	9 30	"	New York..........	479	5 00	A.M.
Bellows Falls......	372	11 45	A.M.	Crawford House....	0	4 30	A.M.
				Profile House......		7 00	"
White R'r Ju'n {ar. lv.	312	1 15 / 1 25	P.M.	Littleton...........	22	9 00	"
				Wells River	42	10 13	"
Wells River	347	3 33	"	White River {ar. Junction.... lv.	77	12 00 / 12 25	M. / P.M.
Littleton..........	367	4 40	"				
Profile House } Wh	379	6 30	"	Bellows Falls. {ar. lv.	117	2 25	"
Crawf'rd H'se } Mts	389	9 30	"	New York..........	389	5 00	A.M.

F. A. HOWELL,

No. 5 NORTH WILLIAM STREET, near Frankfort St., N. Y.

MANUFACTURER OF ALL KINDS OF

SHOW CASES.

Silver Plated, White Metal & Brass Sash Bars
For SHOW WINDOWS made to order at the shortest notice.

BRINLEY & STEEL'S
Hotel and Dining Saloons,
(On the European Plan,)

Nos. 312, 314 & 316 GREENWICH ST.

And 166 READE STREET.

120 Large and Airy Rooms,
BY THE DAY OR WEEK.

Meals as per Bill of Fare.

JAS. STEEL.   W. M. BRINLEY.

Francis & Loutrel,
STATIONERS
AND
PRINTERS,
45 Maiden Lane, New York.

We supply everything in our line at lowest price. Orders solicited.

BENNETT, JOHNSON & CO.,
MANUFACTURERS OF

Cole Fluting Machines,  **and Carriage Hardware,**

476 Broadway, New York.

A. A. CONSTANTINE'S
PERSIAN HEALING, OR PINE TAR SOAP.

For the Toilet this Soap has no equal. It preserves the complexion fair, the skin soft, flexible, and healthy. It removes all Dandruff, preserves the hair soft and silky, and prevents it from falling off.

It cures Pimples on the Face, Cracked or Chapped Hands, Salt Rheum, Frosted Feet, Burns, Fresh Cuts or Wounds of all kinds, all Diseases of the Scalp and Skin, and is a GOOD SHAVING SOAP.

WHAT THOSE SAY WHO USE IT:

"I have used your Soap for Diseases of the Skin, and Catarrh, and have found it superior to any remedial agent I have ever used."
C. S. GOODRICH, M.D., 34 Leroy St., N. Y.

"I can recommend your Persian Healing Soap for *BALDNESS*: it is bringing my hair in beautifully.' I consider it the best Hair Renovator in use."
M. H. COMBS, 218 Atlantic St., Brooklyn, N.Y.

"I have used it for Catarrh in the head, making a suds and snuffing it through the nose, and it has cured me. I use it constantly for the TOILET, and consider it the BEST SOAP FOR THAT PURPOSE."
G. R. BENSON, Office of the U. S. Life Ins. Co., 40 Wall St., N.Y.

"I have used your Persian Healing Soap in my practice extensively, and it has proved the best healing soap I ever used. It has no equal as a soap for washing the heads and skin of children."
L. I. ALDRICH, M.D., 19 Harrison St., N.Y.

Rev. J. R. ADAMS, Pastor of the M.E. Church, Bloomfield, N. J., writes: "Of your Persian Healing Soap I can speak with confidence, and in high eulogy. 'It is a charm.' It heals with unusual rapidity. I don't want to be without it," &c.

J. H. T. KING, Member of the Royal College of Surgeons, England, writes: "It gives me pleasure to certify to the good qualities of your Soap I use it for the Toilet and Bathing, and prefer it to any other."

The wife of Rev. Dr. KING, Missionary at Athens, Greece, writes: "I have used your Soap for Rheumatism, and find it exceedingly good, and recommend it to all."

"YOUR PERSIAN HEALING SOAP WILL CURE SALT RHEUM. I had it very badly fifteen years, and your Soap has made a complete cure."
G. M. PRALL, 119 West St., N.Y.

"It accomplishes all it claims."
R. HAMILTON, M.D., Saratoga, N. Y.

A. A. CONSTANTINE & CO., 43 Ann St., N Y.

1869.

Albany and New York
DAY LINE,

ON THE HUDSON RIVER.

SUMMER ARRANGEMENT FOR PLEASURE TRAVEL.

THE STEAMBOATS

C. VIBBARD AND DANIEL DREW,

Will, on and after May 31st,

LEAVE NEW YORK DAILY,

From Desbrosses Street at 7, and 34th Street at 7.15 A.M., landing at WEST POINT, NEWBURGH, POUGHKEEPSIE, RHINEBECK, CATSKILL, and HUDSON, Connecting at Albany with 4.30 train on the Rensselaer and Saratoga Railroad; the 5 and 11 P. M. trains on the New York Central; and the evening trains on the Susquehanna, to

MONTREAL, SARATOGA,
Buffalo, Niagara Falls, Sharon Springs,

AND ALL POINTS NORTH AND WEST.

Leave Albany at 9 A. M., connecting with Chicago Express on the New York Central to January 1st. On and after January 1st will leave at 10 A. M., or on arrival of the Rensselaer and Saratoga Railroads.

NEW YORK, May 20, 1869.

GREAT IMPROVEMENT AND REVOLUTION IN

KEROSENE LIGHTS.

New Houses furnished Complete, and Old-fashioned Lamps improved or superseded by

IVES' PATENT LAMP

REDUCED PRICES

The safest and most convenient Lamp ever used.

CHANDELIERS, BRACKETS,

Hanging and Table Lamps, of all kinds, can be lighted as quickly as Gas, filled and trimmed safely and neatly, all without removing the Shade, Globe or Chimney, or unscrewing the Burner.

We have in Stock a complete assortment of Foreign and Domestic

KEROSENE LAMPS & FIXTURES.

Also, a choice selection of first-class

GAS CHANDELIERS,

Fitted with our improvements for oil, and specially adapted for suburban residences which have been or are to be piped for gas, but to which the mains have not yet reached, and oil is to be used temporarily; or they can be used elsewhere as well.

NO ONE NEED BE IN THE DARK!

ALL TRAVELLERS SHOULD USE THE

Pocket Lantern

VERY LIGHT, STRONG, AND DURABLE. Can be folded and carried in the pocket or travelling bag with safety and convenience, occupying the space of a cigar case, and are opened and closed as readily. They contain, whether open or closed, matches and extra candles, and, being always ready for use, ARE MOST APPRECIATED IN THE GREATEST EMERGENCIES.

JULIUS IVES & CO.,

37 Barclay St., and 42 Park Place,

Removed from 49 Maiden Lane.   NEW YORK.

"SHORE LINE" EXPRESS ROUTE.

NEW YORK AND BOSTON.

May 10, 1869.   THROUGH TRAINS.

Trains Leave.	A.M.	P.M.	P.M.	Trains Leave.	A.M.	A.M.	P.M.
New York, 27th st.	8 00	12 15	8 00	Boston	11 10	.....	9 00
Stamford	9 26	1 41	9 30	Mansfield	11 58	.....	9 48
					P.M.		
Norwalk	9 44	1 59	9 49	Providence	12 40	7 20	10 30
Bridgeport.......	10 15	2 32	10 33	Greenwich.........	1 00	7 52	10 58
New Haven	10 55	3 15	11 15	Kingston	1 24	8 26	11 24
	P.M.		A.M.				
Connecticut River.	12 30	4 20	12 30	Westerly...........	1 55	9 12	11 58
Lyme.............	12 35	4 30	12 35	Stonington	2 05	9 27	12 09
							A.M.
New London	1 15	5 15	1 15	New London	2 45	11 05	12 40
Stonington.......	2 05	6 04	1 53	Lyme	3 05	11 48	1 14
Westerly..........	2 16	6 15	2 07	Connecticut River..	3 15	12 03	1 20
						P.M.	
Kingston.........	3 00	6 50	2 49	New Haven........	4 30	2 05	2 40
Greenwich........	3 29	7 10	3 20	Bridgeport........	5 05	2 40	3 16
Providence.......	4 15	7 35	4 00	Norwalk	5 39	3 12	3 47
Mansfield	5 05	8 17	4 37	Stamford	6 00	3 32	4 08
Boston	6 10	9 05	5 40	New York, 27th st..	7 20	4 55	5 30

NEW YORK AND BOSTON EXPRESS LINE— SPRINGFIELD ROUTE.

Mls.	A.M.	P.M.	P.M.	*P.M.	May 10, 1869.	A.M.	P.M.	P.M.	A.M.
0	8 00	3 00	8 00	5 00	New York { 27th st..	3 10	4 55	11 20	5 30
2	8 08	3 08	8 08	5 07	{ 42d st...	3 02	4 48	11 12	5 24
36	9 26	4 22	9 30	6 24	Stamford.	.....	3 32	9 56	4 08
44	9 44	4 40	9 49	.....	Norwalk.............	..●..	3 12	9 37	3 47
58	10 15	5 13	10 33	.....	Bridgeport.......	.....	2 40	9 05	3 16
76	10 50	5 50	11 10	.....	arr. { N. Haven { I've	12 28	2 05	8 30	2 40
	10 55	5 55	11 15	7 50	I've { { arr	12 28	2 00	8 30	2 40
94	11 37	6 37	11 57	8 30	Meriden	11 54	1 30	7 59	2 03
101	11 57	6 54	.....	8 48	Berlin...	11 37	1 12	7 41	.....
112	12 23	7 19	12 40	9 12	Hartford.............	11 19	12 50	7 20	1 26
138	1 10	8 05	1 40	.....	arr. { Springfield { I've	10 25	12 00	6 30	12 30
	1 45	8 30	2 00	10 10	I've { { arr.	9 50	11 55	6 15	12 30
153	2 14	8 59	2 32	10 39	Palmer	9 22	11 30	5 48	12 05
167	2 43	9 28	3 04	11 08	West Brookfield.....	8 57	11 05	5 23	11 37
192	3 35	10 20	4 15	11 55	arr. { Worcester. { I've	8 00	10 05	4 30	10 35
	3 40	10 25	4 20	12 00	I've { { arr.	8 00	10 00	4 25	10 30
215	4 21	11 06	5 06	12 48	South Framingham...	7 15	9 15	3 41	9 43
236	5 05	11 50	5 50	1 35	Boston..............	*6 30	8 30	3 00	9 00
	P.M.	P.M.	A.M.	A.M.		P.M.	A.M.	P.M.	P.M.

* Sunday mail.   Through fare, six dollars.

ARCHER & PANCOAST
MANUFACTURING COMPANY,

MANUFACTURERS OF

GAS FIXTURES,

COAL OIL LAMPS, CHANDELIERS, &c.

OF EVERY DESCRIPTION.

———∾∾———

MANUFACTORY AND WAREROOMS,

9, 11, 13 MERCER ST., NEW YORK.

———∾∾———

N. B.—Designs for special purposes, such as PUBLIC HALLS, MEDIÆ-VAL, and ARCHITECTURAL CHURCH FIXTURES, ECCLESIASTICAL EMBLEMS, MASONIC LODGES, &c., submitted on short notice.

NORWICH LINE

TO

BOSTON.

VIA

NEW LONDON, NORWICH, AND WORCESTER,

AND TO THE

WHITE MOUNTAINS,

VIA

NEW LONDON, NORWICH, WORCESTER, NASHUA, CONCORD, PLYMOUTH, WELLS RIVER,

LITTLETON.

OR

LAKE WINNIPISEOGEE.

Steamer CITY OF BOSTON, ... Capt. WILLIAMS,
" CITY OF NEW YORK, . . . " JEWETT,
" CITY OF LAWRENCE, . . . " LAMPHEARE,
" CITY OF NEW LONDON, . . . " LADD,
" CITY OF NORWICH, ... " BROWN,

two of which leave Pier 40, North River, alternately, at 5 P.M. in the summer, and 4 P.M. in the winter, connecting at New London with Express trains for all the above points.

Express passenger train leaves Boston & Albany Railroad station, corner Beach and Lincoln streets, at 5.30 P.M., connecting with Express train at Worcester from the White Mountains, reaching steamboat about 10 P.M., where passengers will find the comforts of a first-class hotel.

P. S. M. ANDREWS, *Superintendent*, Norwich.
A. FIRTH, *Assistant-Superintendent*, Boston.
C. S. TURNER, *Superintendent*, Worcester.
J. R. KENDRICK, *Superintendent*, Concord.
J. A. DODGE, *Superintendent*, Plymouth.
JULIUS WEBB, *General Manager*, Norwich, and N. Y. Transpt. Co., Norwich.
E. S. MARTIN, *Agent*, Pier 40, North River, N. Y.

THE PATENT
ARION PIANO-FORTE
COVELL & CO., 554 BROADWAY, N. Y.

Trade Mark—Copyrighted.

A complete assortment of these CELEBRATED INSTRUMENTS, patented by MR. GEORGE C. MANNER, always on hand.

THE FAIR OF THE AMERICAN INSTITUTE,

Held in New York in 1867, when all the first-class Pianos were on exhibition, and after a severe test trial, declared the "ARION" to be THE BEST.

It supersedes all others on account of its *great strength, evenness of action, purity of vibration, and elegance of finish ;* and not least of all,

WILL STAND IN TUNE LONGER THAN ANY OTHER.

We invite all lovers of the finest of parlor instruments call and examine for themselves.

COVELL & CO., 544 Broadway

N. B.—AGENTS WANTED.

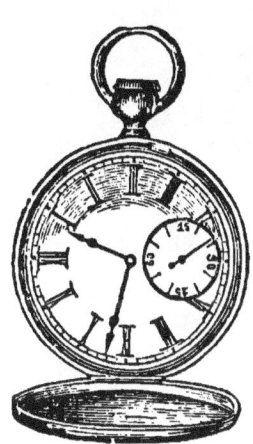

$12. $15. $20.
THE CELEBRATED GENUINE
"OROIDE WATCHES"

resemble Gold, wear like Gold, and are AS GOOD AS GOLD in all respects, except intrinsic value—COSTING ONLY ONE-SIXTH AS MUCH.

Every Watch Guaranteed
BY SPECIAL CERTIFICATE.

CHAINS AND JEWELRY

IN ALL VARIETIES.

Call and Examine for Yourselves.

☞ *Remember, the only* GENUINE OROIDE WATCHES *can be got of*

JAMES GERARD & CO.,
SOLE AGENTS FOR THE UNITED STATES,

85 Nassau Street (Up Stairs), New York.

DEPOT OF GAMES.

FREE DIRECTIONS for Playing the Games of EUCHRE, WHIST, BEZIQUE, SEVEN-UP, CRIBBAGE, BOSTON, POKER, CHESS, CHECKERS, BACKGAMMON, AND ALL OTHER GAMES.

Either of the above and our Mammoth Catalogue of Games sent to any address free upon receipt of postage (4 cents). Address,

CRAWFORD & DAVIDSON,
No. 38 JOHN ST., N. Y. City.

THE AUTOMATIC CLOTHES-WASHER & BOILER.
JOHN REIST, Pat. Nov. 29, 1864.

Dispenses with labor, wear, and tear. Decided by the Patent Office to be the only original and first Self-Acting Portable Wash-Boiler ever made. (See Decision of the United States Patent Office, Nov. 3, 1868.)

Liberal terms offered to Dealers and reliable Agents.

SEND STAMP FOR CIRCULAR.

From Journal New York State Fair, 1868.
"The operation of this machine was fully satisfactory, and the Committee *award it the First Premium,* for the reason that it did its work effectually without rubbing the clothes."

Sample Boiler, No. 8, medium size, $10; or parts for the improvement, which can be made to fit any Boiler, with Royalty stamp, $4. Sent C. O. D.

AUTOMATIC CLOTHES-WASHER & BOILER CO.
Depot, 19 Courtlandt St., New York.

Saratoga Spring Co.

SARATOGA SPRINGS, N. Y.

A. PUTNAM, Jr., Sup't.

ANALYSIS BY . . . . . . PROF. C. F. CHANDLER.

Chloride of Sodium,	378.962 grs.
Chloride of Potassium,	9.229 "
Bromide of Sodium,	.565 "
Iodide of Sodium, or Iodine,*	20.000 "
Sulphate of Potassa,	5.500 "
Bicarbonate of Lime,	124.459 "
Bicarbonate of Magnesia,	61.912 "
Bicarbonate of Soda,	12.662 "
Bicarbonate of Iron,	1.213 "
Silica	1.283 "
Phosphate of Lime, a trace.	
Solid Contents in a gallon,	615.685 grs.

Carbonic Acid Gas, 407.55 cubic inches in a gallon.

* Ascertained according to Dr. Steele and Professor Emmons' mode of Analysis.

TESTIMONIALS.

The following testimonials of the value of the Star Water, are selected from many received from those who have used the water:

From Rev. THEODORE L. CUYLER, D. D.

Saratoga Springs, N. Y., Aug. 15, 1867.

After eighteen years of constant experience in the use of the Saratoga Waters, I do not hesitate to give the preference to the STAR SPRING as the most active and beneficial cathartic I have ever found here. It "works like a charm." I keep a supply of it at my own home, and when my system becomes disordered, and my liver grows sluggish in its action, a bottle or two of this capital water restores me without the use of any other remedy. May yours be "the *Star* that never sets."

Faithfully yours, - THEODORE L. CUYLER.

From J. S. DELAVAN, M.D.

Albany, May 9, 1865.

SARATOGA STAR SPRING CO.—*Gents:* I am in receipt of your admirable water. As a REMEDIAL AGENT, I believe the Star Water to be greatly superior to any of the mineral waters of Saratoga. I greatly prefer it myself to any of them.

Very truly yours, J. S. DELAVAN, M.D.

From Dr. N. B. SHURTLEFF, Mayor of Boston.

Boston, Oct. 18. 1867.

The Saratoga Spring Water has proved highly advantageous in my practice in relieving constitutional torpidity of the alimentary canal, I consider its use very valuable in the treatment of Chronic Indigestion, in reducing scrofulous enlargements, and in removing cutaneous affections. NATH. B. SHURTLEFF, M.D.

WHOLESALE AGENTS:

I. WHITE & CO., 100 Tremont Street, Boston.
B. HOWARD & SON, 94 Reade Street, New York.
HARRIS & UPHAM, 72 Randolph Street, Chicago, Ill.
JOHN WYETH & BROTHER, 1412 Walnut Street, Philadelphia.
BROWN, WEBER & GRAHAM, 10 & 12 North Second St., St. Louis.

And principal Druggists generally.

TAINTOR'S ROUTE AND CITY GUIDES.

These GUIDES describe all CITIES, TOWNS and STATIONS on the routes, giving items of interest to the traveller for business or pleasure, and

HANDSOMELY COLORED AND VERY PERFECT MAPS,

enabling the traveller at every part of his journey to mark his precise locality, and recognize the surrounding scenery.

- I.—"CITY OF NEW YORK" GUIDE.
- II.—"NEW YORK TO PHILADELPHIA, BALTIMORE, AND WASHINGTON."
- III.—"HUDSON RIVER" GUIDE.
- IV.—"HUDSON RIVER RAILWAY" GUIDE.
- V.—"ERIE RAILWAY" GUIDE.
- VI.—"NEW YORK TO SARATOGA, BUFFALO, AND NIAGARA FALLS."
- VII.—"NEW YORK CENTRAL RAILWAY."
- VIII.—"SPRINGFIELD ROUTE." New York to Boston. via Springfield.
- IX.—"SHORE LINE ROUTE" GUIDE. New York to Boston.
- X.—"BRISTOL LINE" GUIDE. New York to Boston, via Bristol.
- XI.—"STONINGTON LINE." New York to Boston, via Stonington.
- XII.—"NORWICH LINE." New York to Boston and White Mountains.
- XIII.—"NEW YORK TO MONTREAL." Route via New London.
- XIV.—"NEW YORK TO WHITE MOUNTAINS, via CONNECTICUT RIVER."
- XV.—"THE NORTHERN ROUTE" GUIDE. Boston to White Mountains, Montreal, and Ogdensburg.
- XVI.—"HARLEM ROUTE" GUIDE.
- XVII.—"ALLENTOWN LINE" GUIDE. New York to Harrisburgh.
- XVIII.—"PENNSYLVANIA COAL REGIONS, via MORRIS AND ESSEX R. R.
- XIX.—"LONG ISLAND," via Long Island Railroad.
- XX.—"THE SOUND ROUTES TO BOSTON."

Other Routes will soon be published.

TAINTOR'S "CITY OF NEW YORK"

Contains descriptions of, and directions for visiting the PUBLIC BUILDINGS, PARKS, CEMETRIES, ISLANDS, and PUBLIC INSTITUTIONS in and around New York City; also contains lists of the principal Hotels, Places of Amusement, Libraries, Clubs, Societies, Dispensaries, Horse Railroads, Omnibus Routes, Hack Fares, Ferries, &c; also,

A NEW STREET DIRECTORY,
TRAVELLERS' DIRECTORY AND CHURCH DIRECTORY,

AND A

LARGE COLORED MAP
OF
NEW YORK, BROOKLYN, JERSEY CITY, HOBOKEN, &c.

Price, 25 cents. For Sale by Newsdealers and Booksellers.

TAINTOR BROTHERS, Publishers, 678 Broadway, N. Y.

MIDDLETOWN HEALING SPRINGS,

MIDDLETOWN, RUTLAND CO., VERMONT.

(Railroad Station, Poultney.)

The attention of tourists, and invalids particularly, is directed to these Springs, whose waters are very highly recommended by Physicians and all others familiar with *their wonderful effect on disease.* They are UNRIVALLED as a *Remedy*, refreshing as a Beverage, and pronounced

SUPERIOR TO ALL OTHER WATERS.

The location is delightful and healthy, and the region abounds with beautiful scenery, splendid drives, fine fishing, &c., &c.

The Waters are *free* to all at the Springs, and *bottled for shipping*, and sold by Druggists.

Send for Pamphlets; full particulars free.

Address, GRAYS & CLARK,
Middletown, Vermont.

RIPLEY FEMALE COLLEGE,
Poultney, Vt.
REV. J. NEWMANN, D.D., President.

This well-established Institution, located in a most delightful and healthful region, affords the best of facilities for acquiring a thorough and complete education. Particular attention is given to the Ornamental Branches, and eminent Professors are employed in each of these departments. The Conservatory method of instruction in Music is pursued with those who desire it. Prof. H. C. Treat, from the Alleghany Academy of Music, has been engaged to introduce the method of instruction pursued so successfully at that Institution. The Fall Term begins September 15th.

On the 12th of July, 1869, this Institution is opened as

A SUMMER RESORT.

It combines more elements of comfort than are usually found from home. The building is of brick, and is isolated from other buildings. Being in the centre of ten acres of lawn and grove, it is removed from noise and dust, and is emphatically *a Cool Retreat.* The gravel roads for miles in all directions are superior to macadamized roads. The scenery is of mountains, valleys, streams, and lakes, rarely equalled. At ordinary summer resorts the rule is the minimum of comforts and the maximum of prices. Here the rule is reversed.

Prices for board, from $8 to $12 per week, according to size and position of rooms.

For children under twelve years of age, and for servants, $7 per week. Transient boarders, $2.50 per day.

MIDDLETOWN WATER FURNISHED FREE.

How Shall we Paint our Houses?

READY-MADE COLORS
For Painting Exteriors and Interiors of Country and City Houses.

These Paints require only to be thinned with Raw Linseed Oil to make them ready for use. The list includes forty shades and tints, comprising all the colors suitable for exterior and interior painting. In durability and permanency of color they will be found superior in every respect to pure White Lead, while they cost (considering the quantity required) only about half as much.

Sample Cards, with a descriptive pamphlet, sent free by mail. Be sure you get the genuine *"Railroad"* Colors, every package of which bears our full name, in addition to our copyrighted title,

"Railroad Paints and Railroad Colors.

☞ *None are reliable which do not bear these marks.* ☜

We would call attention also to our

Warranted Perfectly Pure Combination White Lead,

which, for economy and durability, is the best in market. For sale by all Paint Dealers throughout the country, or

MASURY & WHITON,
111 Fulton Street, N. Y.

Proprietors of the Globe White Lead and Color Works, Manufacturers of White Lead, Zinc, and Painters' Fine Colors.

N.B.—"HOW SHALL WE PAINT?" A popular treatise on the art of House Painting, &c., by JOHN W. MASURY. Cloth. 216 pages, $1.50. Also, HINTS ON HOUSE PAINTING. Cloth, 84 pages, 40 cents. Either of the above sent free by mail on receipt of price.

CARMINA YALENSIA.

A New Collection of COLLEGE SONGS, with MUSIC and PIANO-FORTE ACCOMPANIMENTS, comprising all the old popular and standard College Songs, with numerous pieces not hitherto published. The famous "WOODEN SPOON LANCIERS," and the "SONG OF THE SPOON;" also, the celebrated "CHRISTMAS ANTHEM," sung by the Beethoven Society of Yale, are included. Extra cloth, price $1.50. Mailed post-paid on receipt of price.

TAINTOR BROTHERS, Publishers,
678 BROADWAY, NEW YORK.

THE CATSKILL MOUNTAINS,
And the Region Around.

THEIR SCENERY, LEGENDS, AND FEATURES.

With sketches in prose and verse by COOPER, IRVING, BRYANT, COLE, and other eminent writers. By REV. CHARLES ROCKWELL. Illustrated. One volume 12mo, extra cloth, 350 pages, $2.00.

TAINTOR BROTHERS, Publishers,
678 BROADWAY, NEW YORK.

HEAR YE! HEAR YE!

Hearken, all ye lean and gaunt,
That racking Nervous Headaches haunt.
Give ear, give ear, ye Bilious crowds,
Whose cheeks the saffron bile-tinge clouds.
Attend, attend, ye sore depressed,
Who can't the simplest food digest—
To you is proffered such a draught
As Hebe's patrons never quaffed;
Ease, Health, and Strength 'twill soon restore,
And, stepping backward from Death's door,
You'll bless the skilful hand that blent
The Seltzer's every element
In one rare antidote, containing
Help, sure and swift, for the complaining.

PREPARED ONLY BY

TARRANT & CO.,
273 Greenwich Street, N. Y.

SOLD BY ALL DRUGGISTS.

MERIDEN CUTLERY CO.

MANUFACTURERS OF SUPERIOR

TABLE CUTLERY,

Of PEARL, IVORY, HORN, BONE, EBONY, and COCOA HANDLES.

Also, Exclusive Manufacturers of the Patent

HARD RUBBER HANDLE,

Which is the most DURABLE Handle ever known.

It is much less expensive than IVORY.
It always retains its polish when in use.
It is Warranted NOT TO BECOME LOOSE in the Handle.
It is not affected by HOT WATER.

A NEW THING!!

Solid Cast-Steel Knife,

Heavily Silver-Plated.

PATENTED APRIL, 1867.

☞ For sale by all the principal Dealers in Cutlery throughout the United States, and by the

MERIDEN CUTLERY CO.,

45 Beekman Street, New York.

NORTH AMERICA
Life Insurance Company,
229 BROADWAY,
Corner of Barclay Street.
N. D. MORGAN, President.

This Company offers better inducements to insurers than any other in the United States. NO LIMITATION TO TRAVEL, at any season of the year, in any part of North America, north of Mexico, or in Europe.

Policies Secured by Special Pledge of Public Stocks

in the Insurance Department of the State of New York, and each REGISTERED POLICY will bear a CERTIFICATE to that effect, countersigned by the SUPERINTENDENT OF THE INSURANCE DEPARTMENT.

This feature of security originated with this Company, and was the invention of its present President. Nearly *five millions* of its policies are already secured in this manner. Communications addressed to the principal office, or to any of its agencies, will be promptly attended to.

J. W. MERRILL, Secretary.

www.ingramcontent.com/pod-product-compliance
Lightning Source LLC
Chambersburg PA
CBHW031122160426
43192CB00008B/1076